SOME NINETEENTH CENTURY GARDENERS

BY THE SAME AUTHOR

IT WAS NOT JONES (Poems), Hogarth Press

INSECT LIFE IN BRITAIN (Britain in Pictures), Collins

SOME BRITISH BEETLES, Penguin Books

ENGLISH LANDSCAPE, An Anthology (with
    John Betjeman), Muller

Till 1930; G. Phills.
cf. M. Seymour-Smith, Robt Graves, p. 155 ff

Some Nineteenth Century Gardeners

Geoffrey Taylor

Philip Gough.

Skeffington

First published 1951

Printed in Great Britain
by The Anchor Press, Ltd.,
Tiptree, Essex

DEDICATION

NOTE

THE writing of this book has brought me in debt to many friends, but particularly to Reginald Ross Williamson, and to Lady Moore who, besides giving me invaluable information, has been as generous with her time as she is with her plants.

G. T.

CONTENTS

"The art of gardening. In this the artist who lays out the work, and devises a garment for a piece of ground, has the delight of seeing his work live and grow hour by hour; and, while it is growing, he is able to polish, to cut and carve, to fill up here and there, to hope and to love."

ALBERT, Prince-Consort of England.

LIST OF ILLUSTRATIONS

THE hundred years or so from Queen Anne to Queen Victoria was, as everyone agrees, the Age of Reason. Among the many matters which its sophisticated dilettanti reasoned on was a question of gardens. In a proper garden does Art or does Nature predominate? In a way it was a silly question—like many others that they asked. Behind it lay the classical assumption that by some accepted measure or standard a proper garden might be known— an assumption that was colourable only when applied to poetry or painting or one of the other Arts, and which therefore presupposed the answer to the question they were asking. "I believe it is no wrong observation," said Pope, talking of gardens, "that persons of genius are always most fond of Nature. On the contrary, people of the common level of understanding are principally delighted with the little niceties and fantastical operations of Art."

One may agree with him, while noting that the question is begged *ad hominem*; and agree more readily with Addison who could not but "fancy that an Orchard in flower looks infinitely more delightful than all the little labyrinths of the most finished Parterre". These men were urbane in every sense of the word. At the other end of the century there is Repton in the rising tide of the Romantic Revival, and himself, in practice, a "naturalist", declaring that "Gardens are works of Art rather than of Nature"; and quoting Burke, that "Designs that are vast only by their dimensions are always the signs of a common and low imagination. No work of Art can be great but as it deceives, to be otherwise is the prerogative of Nature only."

Actually the position at which eighteenth century practice more or less settled was indicated by the poet Mason's "ingenious and learned friend", Dr. Burgh, when he remarked that "Gardening imparts to rural scenery what a noble and graceful deportment confers upon the human frame"—a statement that left plenty of room for varied interpretation.

The same question, however, cropped up again in the nineteenth century: but then it was answered on a more frankly emotional basis. For the two ages, though we now see that there was more continuity of tradition between them than the later nineteenth century itself supposed, were yet different in temperament and outlook. This showed itself in gardening as in all else.

In the eighteenth century the English garden was an affair of wide prospects, of views and vistas, of incorporating and modifying the entire landscape, including the children of the local peasantry—"arming the infant shepherds with the proper implements of their picturesque office". The great gardeners were many of them architects become almost geographers—Vanbrugh, Kent, Chambers —playing with woods, and waters, and fields of a hundred acres; the lesser men among them creating all too often "designs that were vast only by their dimensions".

In the nineteenth century, gardening activities, though they were still conceived with a spacious sweep, began to be somewhat contracted. The population was increasing and the social emphasis was shifting. Landscape gardening persisted, but of course on a smaller scale, with a diminished perspective, in the innumerable villa gardens of the rising middle class. The characteristic Victorian gardener, the sort of man who influenced garden trends, is no architect, but more likely than not a country clergyman—a Canon Ellacombe or a Dean Hole.

But indeed, in that almost mythical period there were

many sorts of garden and many sorts of gardener, from the Dukes of Devonshire remodelling Chatsworth with domed glass and quilted parterre, to Lancashire weavers creating new species, almost, of pansy and auricula. But in all this flux and change, the norm was to be found in the gardens of country rectories and manor-houses—setting a standard for the as yet uncramped demesne of the new city business man in his new suburban villa.

It was this new and increasing class of prosperous and socially competitive amateurs, the cream of the Industrial Revolution, that created a demand for domestic gardeners; a demand which, even in an age when, according to the Prince Consort, private servants were more numerous than any other class in the community, often outran the supply. So that, for this among other reasons, the amateurs in person, particularly the wives and daughters, found themselves taking the flower garden or a fair part of it into their own hands. "I may as well garden a bit," said Miss Rhoda Broughton's Nell Le Strange in the early eighteen-sixties, "it will pass the time." So, with her own fair hands she "fetched a pair of gardening gloves and a little mat, and knelt down on the latter, and set to digging, and raking, and weeding with a will," and, "as she grubbed, and watered, and scuffled, she ran over in her mind all the little incidents of her late dissipation".

Three generations earlier, Marianne Dashwood, for all her love of autumn leaves and her landscape sensibility, would never have dreamed of actually digging. But Miss Broughton's heroine, since she found in her industry "a new and delightful sensation", might, if she could give her mind to the job, become an accomplished gardener. In any case, it was for her and the likes of her that an extensive garden literature grew up.

The best of this literature was produced by men and

women who were gardeners of a creative enthusiasm sometimes amounting to genius—though of course gardening
genius may have been possessed at least as fully by
gardeners who never wrote a word about their work.
But of that one can hardly be sure. For gardening is a
transitory art: more transitory than most. At best a
garden will but by a few years outlive its creator. More
likely, in our day at any rate, six months' neglect will
obliterate the work of sixty years. One can encourage
plants to grow, and one can discourage them; but no
way has yet been discovered, thank goodness and—with
laboratory hydroponics upon us—touching wood, no way
has been discovered of stopping them even when they are
weeds; nor of maintaining them at just the point of
desired perfection. Even the Japanese, working through
experimental centuries with oriental patience, have done
the trick only with a few dwarf trees. Nor have the
Americans with wealth and chemistry done more.

For the rest—Nature creeps on, preventing us from
reassessing the gardeners of the past as we can reassess
the poets and the painters. Not by their gardens, that is.
But if they happen to have left plans or to have written
books about their work, then we have something to
judge them by. They may even stray from the ranks of
the gardeners into those of the men-of-letters—adding a
verbal to their vegetable art.

The number of these literary or, at least, literate
gardeners is very large. In the following chapters I have
written about a few of them whose gardening ability and
picturesque character have roused my own admiration
and interest. My information has been gathered through
years of casual reading in old books and long-forgotten
journals, and in conversation with those who knew
much more than I did. Such reading and conversation
are a way of escape to a carefully selected past, especially

in winter, from our rather cramped atomic present—a present in which what once were acres are shrunk to roods and perches, even to square yards, even to back yards; and our gardens, perhaps, to a couple of narrow beds under our windows or beside the pathway to our door; yet leaving enough, even so, and so far, to occupy us from the beginning of March to the end of November, if we so please.

I have chosen to write of the Loudons and William Robinson and Reginald Farrer because, unlike for instance Paxton or Miss Jekyll, they do not possess full-length biographies, and therefore even the slight sketches I have attempted had to be put together from wherever I could gather information. A good deal of this information I have already used in Third Programme broadcasts.

CHAPTER I

JOHN CLAUDIUS LOUDON AND HIS WIFE JANE

GARDENING, of course, has been a continuous process—as have all other fundamental human activities—
from the Garden of Eden down to the latest thing in
hormone culture. But for convenience, we divide up
these continuous processes, even the very flux of time, into
conventional periods, into schools, trends, tendencies, and
fashions. John Claudius Loudon, himself a passionate
pigeonholer and classifier, was always doing it. For him
"modern gardening" began with the beginning of the
eighteenth century, some two generations before his own.
And doubtless, like the rest of us, he thought of his own
time as being a time of transition.

This sense of living at a critical moment in history
is, most often, an illusion. Yet to us there can be no
question that the last years of the eighteenth and the early
years of the nineteenth centuries really were a meeting, a
mingling, and above all, a troubling, of the waters. In

poetry, not to say anything of politics or economics, Crabbe and Rogers successfully overlapped Wordsworth and Keats. And, considering Gray's opinion that gardening was the only proof of original talent that the English could put forward, surely gardeners need not be placed so far behind poets.

In any case, for us, modern gardening may well be considered as beginning with Loudon himself. As a gardener, he was the genius of a true transition period. And he was, besides, a good deal more than a gardener —a naturalist, a landscape-painter, an architect, and a traveller—but at all times his main interest was in gardening.

Loudon, like so many great Englishmen, was a Scot by birth and parentage. He was born in 1783, the eldest child of a farmer—"a man of enlightened mind and superior information"—who lived at Kerse Hall, some five miles from Edinburgh. Here he laid out his first garden, a small matter of beds and paths, in a plot that his father gave him.

It is likely that learning, book-learning, means more to the Lowlanders of Scotland than to any other people; and at Edinburgh Loudon received a typically Scotch education—liberal and thorough. Writing and drawing, botany and chemistry, Latin and French—these were the subjects that he studied and in which he became proficient: a very different schooling from the purely classical curriculum which is all he could have found anywhere in England at the period: and all of it precisely the sort of schooling which was going to be most useful to him in his subsequent profession.

When he left school Loudon was quite clear as to what that profession should be, and at his own urgent request his father apprenticed him first to one and then to another nurseryman and landscape gardener. And then, with his apprenticeship complete at the age of twenty, in the best Scottish tradition he set out for London. In London he was introduced to John Sowerby, the greatest of all botanical illustrators, and to Sir Joseph Banks, the President of the Royal Society, who was a collector of plants and a patron of collectors, and one of the most enthusiastic gardeners of his time.

It may seem strange that a gardener's apprentice should have had introductions to two such important people, but this again marks a difference between the Scot and an Englishman of comparable status in the year 1803. In Sowerby, Loudon found an acquaintance who encouraged his own innate passion for orderly arrangement, classification, and the filing of documents and papers. With Sir Joseph Banks he formed a more intimate friendship, and one may suppose that Loudon made frequent use of the unrivalled scientific library that Banks had formed in his house at Soho Square and also visited his famous garden at Spring Grove, Isleworth. It was Banks who, soon after his coming to London, secured his election to the Linnean Society.

There is no reason for thinking that all this went in any extent to Loudon's head, but certainly his self-confidence was unmodified by feelings of national or social inferiority, and he looked about him with a critical eye. At that time the public squares in London were entirely planted with the more sombre sort of ever-green—yews, pines, and spruce. Loudon published an article called *Observations on Laying out the Public Squares of London*. I have not been able to trace this article. He himself long afterwards said that it appeared in the *Literary Journal* for 1803—a lapse of memory which has misled many subsequent writers, including his wife and the author of the article on him in the *Dictionary of National Biography*. However, there is no doubt that the paper in question was written and printed soon after his migration from Scotland, and that in it he advised the use of plane-trees, sycamores, and almonds instead of the funereal conifers. I do not know how long it was before his advice was fully adopted. Real improvements, if they were sufficiently obvious, were carried out more quickly in those days than they are now, and certainly the streets and squares of London were transformed within his lifetime.

From urban arboriculture, Loudon's imagination was diverted to other aspects of town planning, some of which had less connexion with the gardener's art. Among his pioneer proposals was a demand for what he called "breathing zones" or unoccupied spaces half a mile broad around London—in fact more than a hundred years ago he was advocating what we now call the "green belt" system. At the same time—in the twenties of last century—he was sounding an alarm about the loss to land fertility through the rapid increase of main drainage schemes—a loss which still causes occasional concern to our far-sighted agriculturalists. His life-long preoccupation with these and other practical problems underlines the strongly utilitarian element in Loudon's character.

It was this strongly practical and methodical bent which attracted him to such unlikely contemporaries as the philosopher, Jeremy Bentham, whose dry bones, preserved in the museum of London University, can hardly be dryer than his dry spirit preserved in—perhaps preserving—the London School of Economics. It was this same methodical bent that enabled him to make and save money. He was in any case a professional success both as a landscape gardener and as a writer. He also dabbled in landscape painting, and his pictures, if they made little direct addition to his bank account, were at least exhibited at the Royal Academy.

There can, in fact, be no question but that Loudon,

J. C. Loudon

Lithograph frontispiece to *Self-Instruction for Young Gardeners*.
J. C. Loudon, 1845

if he was something of a utlitarian, was also rather more than something of an artist—and in more than one medium. I have never seen any of his original paintings, but his drawings as they are reproduced in his numerous books are always deft and lucid. In his writing, like nearly every one of his time, he took trouble and tried to do it well—and he succeeded. Above all, as a landscape gardener he early showed not only a natural good taste in his own work but also a discriminating judgment when discussing the work of others. By this combination of artist with man of business he had, before 1812, saved over £15,000.

Loudon determined to spend some of these considerable savings in foreign travel, and he took advantage of the breathing space in the Napoleonic wars which reopened the Continent to English visitors in 1813. He was well equipped for travelling through Europe, linguistically at least, for, since leaving school where he had been taught French, he had taught himself both German and Italian.

He set out in the middle of March, sailing first to Sweden, where the roads and the educational system pleased him. But he had an Englishman's love of battle-fields and he pushed on to East Prussia, a country where fighting had been recent, plentiful, and bloody. His account of what he saw is pretty well what it might have been had he gone there a century and a quarter later— "Everywhere traces of war: skeletons of horses lay bleaching in the fields, the roads were broken up, and the country houses in ruins." At Elbing the streets were "filled with the goods and cattle of country people who had poured into the town for protection", and southward near Marienburg he ran into "a bivouac of 2,000 Russian troops, who in their dress and general appearance looked more like convicts than soldiers".

None the less, this unfavourable impression made by the Russian soldiery did not deter him from some months later entering Russia—which was not particularly easy even in those days. Behind the iron curtain of that secretive and suspicious land he had many adventures. At one place he was attacked by Cossacks who wanted to eat his horses and who were beaten off by the whips of his coachman and servants. At another place he had to sleep in his carriage, covered with hay against the Russian cold, only to be awakened in the Russian darkness by a herd of cows in the act of eating his covering. On his way to St. Petersburg, after being arrested as a spy for sketching a ruined castle, his carriage stuck in a snowdrift where his coachman and servants, less brave than when faced with Cossacks, rode off on the carriage horses leaving Loudon to the wolves which howled around him all night hoping to eat him in that hungry country. However, as his wife long afterwards said, "Few men were better fitted by nature for bearing the horrors of such a night."

Besides warlike sight-seeing and odd dietetic adventures, Loudon on this tour continued in full pursuit of his profession. He visited every garden he could hear of on or near his proposed route. He also called on every man of learned or scientific eminence in the towns that he passed through. So much did he himself impress these learned men that he was elected a member of the Imperial Society of Moscow, the Natural History Society of Berlin, and the Royal Economical Society of Potsdam. Of Russian gardens and gardeners he formed a poor opinion. He was equally contemptuous of the bad taste of the nobles and of the degradation of their slaves. He found no native gardeners, but the more wealthy of the upper class imported foreigners, English or German, by whose horticultural pretensions they were readily impressed.

Loudon just missed Capability Brown's disciple, Gould, the most famous of these foreign head-gardeners, who was employed by the great and sinister Gregory Alexandrovitch Potemkin. Gould had returned to his native Ormskirk in Lancashire about the time that Loudon set out on his travels, and he died there at an advanced age in 1816. In Moscow, however, he had left at least a non-horticultural reputation behind him. "This man," wrote Loudon, "had a character in some degree analogous to that of his master; he lived in splendour, kept horses and women, and gave occasionally entertainments to the nobility." He goes on to regret "that even the moral sense of Englishmen, who settle in Russia, becomes in time contaminated by the baneful influence of Russian manners"; and he marvels how "a barbarous people may hang together by a sort of tattered moral principle"—"the simple principle of self preservation", implying the minimum of honour and honesty from the first minister to the meanest slave.

These journeyings through Germany and Russia, lasting some eighteen months, were followed two or three years later by an expedition to France and Italy. Again he visited innumerable gardens, collecting notes for his projected *Encyclopaedia of Gardening*. From Genoa he sent home a collection of Orange trees; and at Florence he observed that *Saxifraga crassifolia*—now called *Bergenia crassifolia*—was killed by a slight frost, though at higher altitudes and in more northern latitudes such as Siberia it would withstand great cold. In Venice he collected and kept with great care in a tin can a living plant of the *Vallisnaria* or Eel-grass. He hoped to be the first to introduce this half-hardy aquatic into England. It is one of those curious plants whose complicated reproductive arrangements hasten one's retreat from Darwin back towards Paley. The male flowers develop in the water at the base of the stems whence they float to the surface. There they are joined by the female flowers when these are ready for fertilization. The fertilized females are then drawn back to the muddy bottom by the spiral contraction of their stalks.

It is no wonder that Loudon would let no one else look after his precious specimen. As he himself said, he nursed it as if it had been a child, carrying it against the warmth of his body on mule-back over the Simplon Pass, tending it through Genoa and Strasbourg and at last bringing it to Paris. In Paris disaster overtook it. Vallisnaria was, on the night of her arrival, placed with affectionate forethought outside the window, owing to the exceeding stuffiness of Loudon's hotel bedroom. Everything was done to secure the tin can against possibility of falling. Early next morning, however, though the can indeed remained, Vallisnaria was nowhere to be found—nor was she ever seen again. Loudon always believed that the plant had been carried off by sparrows. In point of fact, the loss mattered less than he then supposed, for someone else unknown to him had introduced *Vellisnaria* to England a few months before he himself got back. In October 1819 Loudon was again in his Bayswater residence, settling down to what is probably his most famous and important work, the *Encyclopaedia of Gardening*.

This remarkable book, containing over twelve hundred pages of small print, took nearly three years in the writing—and no wonder. But when it appeared, its immediate popularity established its author's reputation. In 1823 Loudon followed up the spectacular literary success of his first "Encyclopaedia" with two smaller books—one on the cultivation of the Pine-apple, the other called the *Greenhouse Companion*. Greenhouses and greenhouse cultivation were then entering their time of greatest popularity—a popularity which was to reach its zenith with glazed apotheosis in the Great Exhibition. Three years later he brought out the first number of *The Gardener's Magazine*, which was also the first thing of its kind and which before long was earning him an annual income of £750. In its early numbers he launched an attack on the Horticultural Society, apparently better justified and certainly more effective than William Robinson's attack in his magazine *The Garden* some fifty years later.

Encouraged by what was, on any reckoning, so considerable a financial success, Loudon at the age of forty-seven married Jane Webb, aged twenty-three. Jane herself has described the rather curious circumstances:

"My father died in 1824," she writes, "and finding on the winding up of his affairs that it would be necessary for me to do something for my support, I had written a strange wild novel called *The Mummy*, in which I had laid the scene in the twenty-second century, and attempted to predict the state of improvement to which this country might possibly arrive. Mr. Loudon chanced to see the review of this book in the *Literary Gazette*, and, as among other things, I had mentioned a steam-plough, it attracted his attention, and he procured the work from a circulating library. He read it and was so much pleased with it that he published, in the *Gardener's Magazine* for 1828, a notice of it under the head of 'Hints for Improvements'; and he had from that time a great desire to become acquainted with the author, whom he supposed to be a man. In February, 1830, Mr. Loudon chanced to mention this wish to a lady, a friend of his, who happened to be acquainted with me, and who immediately invited him to a party,

where she promised him he should have the wished-
for introduction. It may be easily supposed that he
was surprised to find the author of the book a woman;
but I believe that from that evening he formed an
attachment to me, and, in fact we were married on
the 14th of the following September."

Fortunate Jane Webb. In 1828 the clouds on the civi-
lized horizon were few and insignificant. The present
was then rich with a promise of future prosperity from
which she and nearly all others had the assurance of
their generation—shared by several generations to come
—that the march of progress would be uninterrupted and
beneficent, even to the predicted production of a steam-
plough. Fortunate she was, in that her faith never saw,
never so much as suspected, its own unfulfilment. Fortunate at least in that, as an unsought side-issue, her
optimism led her into what has all the appearance of
having been an arduous but happy marriage.

Jane Webb had published a small volume of verses
and had proposed to herself a career as a novelist. *The
Mummy* is not really readable today, but it is hardly less
so than any other fantasy of the future, and it contains
passages which suggest an uncommon capacity for specu-
lative thought in its youthful author. The most enlightened
part of society in her twenty-second century believe in
ghosts and hobgoblins "because," as she says, "the ex-
tremes of ignorance and civilization tend alike to produce
credulity". She foresaw the revival of the Roman Catholic
religion and the political separation of Ireland from England—though this last, like the steam-plough, came
sooner than she expected. The steam-plough, indeed, was
to appear but a few years later than her novel, and
well within her own life-time and her husband's.

Though she never became a novelist, Jane Webb

must have been born with some good ink in her veins, for marriage only altered the direction of her literary aim.

"It is scarcely possible," she writes, "to imagine any person more completely ignorant of everything to botany and gardening, than I was at the period of my marriage with Mr. Loudon; and as I found all his family and friends thoroughly acquainted with both subjects, it may be easily conceived that I was soon heartily ashamed of my ignorance, and anxious to remove it as soon as possible."

Her ignorance was not as complete as she here implies. There is evidence in *The Mummy* and in some autobiographical passages in a later book, that she not only had a romantic feeling for gardens, but had had as a child at least some practical experience of gardening. However, compared with her encyclopaedic husband, she was certainly ill-equipped in the science and art to which his life was already dedicated. But when she set out to remedy her defects she soon found that all the available books were either too advanced or else too arbitrary in their instructions—and Jane evidently had the kind of mind that wanted, at every turn, to know "Why?". So she plucked up her womanly courage and approached her husband himself. Here she soon saw that any trepidation, such as she demurely hints at, was all uncalled-for. "He was as anxious to teach me as I was to learn."

Yet even then, under the guidance of the man who was already perhaps the first gardener of the age, it was by no means plain sailing.

"We found unanticipated difficulties at every step; and we both soon discovered the truth of the apparent paradox, that it is not enough to know any

art or science to be able to teach it. It is so very
difficult for a person who has been acquainted with a
subject all his life, to imagine the state of ignorance
in which those are who know nothing of it, that a
professional gardener has rarely patience to teach
anything to an amateur."

Probably Mr. Loudon was not always patient; probably a little of the trepidation was justified after all. Still,
she calls him an "able and never-wearied instructor".
And Jane had other teachers besides her husband. In
particular she attended the lectures of the great Professor
Lindley, the best botanical populariser of the time,
working up her notes into readable and accurate essays
fit for publication in the *Gardener's Magazine*.

So that, one way or another, her difficulties were
overcome. And when she had overcome them they
taught her to write the right kind of books for others who
might be in a like situation, having perhaps less patient
and certainly less learned husbands.

The result was a steady flow of more or less elementary books on Botany and on Gardening, with occasionally
one on Natural History addressed for the most part to
ladies and young people—books written with a lucidity
and good sense that makes them still reliable, and on
many matters, such as the budding of roses, still the
best, guides for beginners.

In Jane Webb, Loudon discovered not only an eager
disciple but, what was more immediately to the point,
an able and willing amanuensis. This might have been,
but probably was not, a matter of the first consideration
with him. For Loudon, by the time of his marriage, was a
one-armed man. Through many years he had suffered
from rheumatism of the right arm; and even more had
he suffered from the "shampooing and stretching" as

they called it, of certain bone-setters whom he consulted. Finally, in 1825, these unskilful practitioners first broke his arm accidentally and then informed him that it must be amputated.

This operation, in the days before anaesthetics as we know them were invented, was described by one of his draughtsmen who was with him on the occasion:

> "Mr. Loudon was a man of great fortitude and unwearied industry. The morning that Doctors Thompson and Lauder called upon him for the purpose of amputating his right arm, they met him in the garden, and asked if he had fully made up his mind to undergo the operation. 'Oh, yes, certainly,' he said; 'it was for that purpose I sent for you'; and added very coolly, 'but you had better step in, and just have a little lunch before you begin.' After lunch he walked up stairs quite composedly, talking to the doctors on general subjects. When all the ligatures were tied, and everything complete, he was about to step down stairs, as a matter of course, to go on with his business; and the doctors had great difficulty to prevail upon him to go to bed."

To a man of Loudon's vigorous self-discipline it would probably have been a small matter, with practice, to have substituted his left hand for his right; but he became afflicted with rheumatism in his left arm also, and to such an extent that he soon had the use of only the third and fourth fingers of his left hand—with which, by the utmost determination, he learned to draw only indifferently. However, nothing damped his ardour. Whilst he was awake he must be working. On his wedding-day, even, whilst his man-servant was dressing him for church, he was all the time dictating to an amanuensis.

It might be supposed then, that Jane Webb was taking on a good deal when she married a man so mentally preoccupied and so physically disabled. She set out, however, to identify herself with his interests, and to make good his functional disability. She would be with him whilst he was directing his labourers on a new site; and always, when they were not working out of doors, there were new books and journals to be written and compiled. Her first job as her husband's right hand was the transcribing at his dictation of the 1,150 pages—in small print, as it appeared when published—of his *Encyclopaedia of Cottage, Farm, and Villa Architecture*.

Jane tells of the prodigious labour involved—of how night after night for many months they sat up working together, never having more than four hours' sleep and drinking strong coffee to keep themselves going. For Loudon, coffee was a substitute for laudanum which he had grown accustomed to during the painful period before his arm was amputated—when he regularly took a wineglassful every eight hours. He cured himself of what he found to be a bad habit by the characteristic method of putting a wineglass of pure water into his two-pint pot of laudanum every time he drew off a wineglass of the drug to drink. In this way the mixture became a little weaker on every occasion and, by the time he was drinking practically plain water, he found himself cured.

The *Encyclopaedia of Cottage Architecture* contains a good deal of gardening advice and information, and in the mere writing of it down Jane Loudon must have learned something about the theoretical aspects of horticulture. On the more practical side her education began in her native city when, a few months after her marriage—on what was practically her honeymoon, in fact—she accompanied her husband to Birmingham, where they spent some six weeks in designing a Botanic Garden. The pair then went on to do a tour of the Lake District and the Scottish Border. They visited at the seats of the nobility and gentry, and entered Loudon's native county of Ayrshire in something like triumphal state—so far was this prophet from being without honour in his own land.

During this northern tour a small cloud appeared in the otherwise clear ointment. This was the first copy, which they bought at Chester, of Paxton's *Horticultural Register*. The *Gardener's Magazine* had been until then without a rival and was providing the Loudons with a handsome income; but the Duke of Devonshire's famous gardener, the apostle of carpet bedding and of the glass-house, the creator of nineteenth-century Chatsworth and the future creator of the Crystal Palace, was either a better editor or a shrewder business man; and Loudon's *Magazine* languished in exact proportion as Paxton's *Register* prospered.

Some time after this, Loudon visited Chatsworth, of which he strongly disapproved—expressing his dis-approval in the pages of the *Gardener's Magazine*. Though Loudon and Paxton were at this time rival editors, there is no need to doubt Loudon's good faith; for though Joseph Paxton—he had not yet been knighted by a grateful Queen—was certainly a man of genius, he was also rather a vulgarian. Indeed it was Paxton's perhaps evil genius that deflected Victorian gardening towards a formal flamboyance which was quite alien to Loudon's conceptions, and from which it was to require a William Robinson to redeem it.

Paxton's well-known good humour did not make him sit down under Loudon's attack, and he defended himself vigorously in his *Horticultural Register*. Thus were fired the first shots of a promising horticultural war. Peace, how-ever, was patched up, and the course of English gardening continued down, not the primrose but the blue lobelia path for at least another forty years. And all because Loudon made the personal acquaintance of Paxton and succumbed to his irresistible charm—so much so that, on a later visit to Chatsworth, he was able to observe there something of actual beauty. Whether or not this involved some compounding with his aesthetic conscience, there is no doubt that in Paxton, Loudon and his wife found a generous and warm-hearted friend.

Paxton killed the *Gardener's Magazine*, though Loudon did not allow it to be buried so long as he himself lived. But the success of his *Encyclopaedia of Cottage Architecture* was so great that in March 1834 he founded the *Architectural Magazine* which, like his *Gardener's Magazine* and his *Magazine of Natural History*, was the first thing of its kind in these Islands. He sold the *Architectural Magazine* in 1838 and the *Magazine of Natural History* a year earlier. It was, incidentally, in the *Magazine of Natural History* for September 1836 that the seventeen-year-old Ruskin, who was afterwards to be the friend of William Robinson, made his first appearance in print.

Of the domestic life of John Claudius and his Jane one does not get many glimpses from which to reconstruct an imaginative picture. Loudon had what almost amounted to a genius for system, for proceeding according to plan. "His love of order was very great," wrote one of his friends. "The books in the library, and manuscripts in his study, were so arranged that he could at any time put his hand upon any book or paper that he might want, even in the dark." One might suppose him none too easy a companion for his wife, to say nothing of little Agnes who was born to them, an only child, some two years after their marriage and who grew up to become herself an author with the publication of *Tales for Young People* in the 1850s. But there is evidence of deep

Loudon's house, Porchester Terrace, Bayswater, 1838

affection between all three members of the Loudon family. They travelled everywhere together—to France and to Scotland again, as well as all over England. And when they were not travelling they lived in their rather gaunt great three-storied home with its lovely garden, the house built to Loudon's own design in 1823 in the select and then still almost rural district of Bayswater.

The house itself, in the newly developed road known as Porchester Terrace, was really half of what Loudon called a "double detached villa". The two houses, costing £5,000 to build, were carefully constructed to look like one—a single house with "some pretensions to architectural design", as Loudon claimed with a certain pride—and this appearance of oneness was continued in the main layout of the two gardens. The Loudons' house looked due south, and contained also the offices of the *Gardener's Magazine*. The garden was most carefully planned, and, though not large, was yet large enough to grow specimens of some 2,000 different kinds of plant species, not counting varieties. It was the garden of a botanist as well as a flower-lover, and it included a sample of seaweeds in a salt-water tank, and a small border devoted to a collection of mosses. The alpine house contained 600 species in small pots, and there was a representative collection of hot-house plants of all the natural orders then in cultivation. In the lawn, making mowing impossible, were between three and four hundred different species of bulbs.

Here Loudon grew his borders of herbaceous plants, his choice shrubs, and his favourite trees; his roses and his vines. Here was his *Lonicera flexuosa* whose sweet scent, when the wind was in the west, greeted him a full quarter mile away as he came home from London—for London had not yet engulfed Porchester Terrace, Bayswater. Until he became financially embarrassed by the publica-

C

tion of his *Arboretum Britannicum* Loudon spent over £250
a year on the upkeep of this quarter-acre garden. It must
have been a pleasant place for a child. Yet her father
cannot have had very much time for little Agnes. One
hopes that there were other children in Bayswater whom
she could invite to play with her in her walled and
wooded garden whilst her father composed his well-
turned ceremonious eighteenth-century phrases, and her
mother wrote them down—rapidly, with a crow quill.

The family idyll, and in its strict and strenuous way
I think it was an idyll, lasted some ten years. Loudon
worked himself to the limit, not knowing when or where
to stop. Between 1835 and 1838 he was engaged on his
ill-fated *Arboretum Britannicum*; and, with his customary
conscientiousness, he determined that all the drawings of
trees must be made direct from nature. To this end he
employed seven artists whose labours he used personally
to superintend—being often out of doors with them from
immediately after his breakfast at 7 a.m. till he came
home for his dinner at eight in the evening; having
remained, as his wife says, "the whole of that time
without taking the slightest refreshment and generally
even without sitting down". Also there were long journeys
to distant and famous trees, groves, or forests.

It was whilst Loudon was carefully collecting facts,
figures, and drawings for his *Arboretum* that a parcel was
one day delivered to the Bishop of London. It came from
the Duke of Wellington, and it contained a pair of
military riding breeches and a curt note in the third
person to the effect that these were the breeches that the
Duke had worn at the Battle of Waterloo. In due course
the garments were returned to the Duke with an equally
cold note in which the Bishop expressed his thanks together with some hint of surprise. It was only then that
Wellington looked once more at a letter still lying on

his table and saw that it was a request that the sender be permitted to inspect the Duke's famous *beeches*—the beech-trees at Strathfieldsaye were old and beautiful— and that the name at the foot of the page was "J. C. Loudon" and *not* the episcopal signature of the scholarly Dr. Blomfield.

Nor did these arduous days, with their occasional *contretemps*, normally end at eight in the evening. After dinner there was the actual writing part of the book to be done, and he and Jane would sit up together till the small hours of the morning. No wonder Loudon's very considerable powers of endurance began to give way.

Moreover, the *Arboretum* when published, though it is still after more than a hundred years recognized and quoted as a first-class authority, was a financial failure. It had cost a great deal of money to produce—there are four volumes of text and another four volumes of beautifully engraved plates—subscriptions had not come up to his ever-sanguine expectation, and in the end Loudon found himself with a debt of some £10,000 which he could not discharge. Many years before this he had given up practising as a professional landscape gardener; but now, though his creditors were not pressing him, he again began to advise on the laying out of gardens and parks—and this in spite of a complaint in his right knee which almost prevented him from walking. His charges were moderate. For a visit within twelve miles of London and not involving his absence for more than eight hours, his fee was five guineas.

His family also rose to the occasion. Two of his sisters learned wood-engraving, so that he need not be at the expense of an engraver for his illustrations—of which all his books carried a prodigal number; and Jane, having, as she said, acquired some knowledge of plants and gardens during the eight years she had acted as his amanuensis, began to write more and illustrate the five beautiful quartos of her *Ladies' Flower Garden of Ornamental Plants*.

In the meantime, Loudon's health was growing steadily worse, and his doctors gave no hope of his recovery. In this state he consulted William Lawrence, F.R.S., the great surgeon and anatomist of St. Bartholomew's Hospital. Lawrence, whose brilliance later earned him a baronetcy, took a different view of the case, and by his skilful treatment restored Loudon to health in a matter of months. In 1839 he began to lay out the *Arboretum* at Derby, which remains, somewhat altered, to the present day. And he also brought out his one-volume edition of the gardening works of Humphry Repton who had died in 1818, and whose successor in many ways Loudon was.

In 1840 the family revisited Paris; and next year they were travelling in Scotland and the North of England. At Manchester Loudon insisted, against Jane's better judgment, in going out in the wet. He caught a cold which turned to a fever at Paisley, where he was in bed at the house of friends for six weeks. Again he recovered, and again he plunged into an orgy of over-work. In 1843 he began to consider the horticultural aspect of graveyards. It was a sombre subject and all too appropriate. During the summer he was engaged to lay out a cemetery at Southampton, and thither he went with his wife and daughter. His febrile obsession with work was, however, impeded by Jane's watchfulness, and he sent her and Agnes back to Bayswater. A fortnight later Jane went down to see him and her first glance told her that this time he really was dying. But his energy was unabated. Having dealt with the Southampton cemetery he went on to tackle one at Bath.

At the end of September he returned to Bayswater, and again consulted Lawrence. Lawrence told him that his lungs were badly affected. At the same time one of his creditors went bankrupt and was obliged to press him for payment. The clouds were gathering blackly around him. He now knew that he was dying but he never for a moment gave in. He sent out an appeal to all the nobility who took an interest in gardening, asking them to buy some of the unsold copies of the *Arboretum*. The response was immediate to the extent of £360—enough to preclude any question of his own bankruptcy. He also worked at top speed to finish his *Self-Instruction for Young Gardeners*. On 14 December he was dictating to Jane. Suddenly he became restless, and walked several times from the drawing-room to his bedroom and back. He appeared to grow weaker. Jane placed her arms around him. And so he died, standing on his feet, dictating with almost his last breath, his head finally resting on his wife's shoulder. It was an heroic and quite characteristic end.

As for Jane, she had many friends. In the Preface to his second volume of *Essays*, dated from Walton Hall, 29 February, 1844, Charles Waterton wrote:

"The volume which I now present to an indulgent public, is an unsolicited donation to the widow of my poor friend Mr. Loudon, whose vast labours in the cause of Science have insured him an imperishable reputation. If this trifling present on my part shall be the medium of conveying one single drop of balm to the wound which it has pleased Heaven lately to inflict on the heart of that excellent lady, my time will have been well employed, and my endeavours amply requited."

The book must have conveyed more than a single drop of balm, for it went through several editions.

One way and another she was able to live on in Bayswater for a further fifteen years, dying there in 1858. She published many more books, all written with her usual clarity and good sense, and some of them are now expensively collected for the sake of their coloured plates. In some of them also, she gives glimpses of her own life. In her teens and apparently after her mother's death, she and her father seem to have moved into the country—presumably back to their ancestral property, Kitwell House, outside Birmingham. "The place we went to live at," she writes, "had a good house, commanding a splendid view; and excellent garden; three fish-ponds, and about thirty acres of land, without troubling us with any of the laborious duties of cultivating arable land." In these attractive surroundings the adolescent Jane Webb looked in a genteel way after her poultry and her flower-garden, and superintended her dairy-maid. Her father would unexpectedly invite callers to stay to dinner, and thus she learned to be far-sighted in her housekeeping.

On her father's death, as we have seen, she took to literature, and thereby met her beloved Mr. Loudon. He and she must have been dissimilar but complementary characters. In his portrait, Loudon has a most attractive face, with a sensitive mouth, a broad forehead, and those round eyes that one notices in such poets as Blake and Clare—poets with a touch of madness. He was a fanatic for truth—sacking one of his servants out of hand for what most people would think the merest peccadillo of a lie. But he was charitable and kind-hearted, and his kindness was easily imposed upon. One of the newspaper obituaries said of him that he was an excellent husband. In a way, I suppose he may have been. Anyhow, it is clear that Jane was devoted to him, and that she was, beyond any doubt, an excellent wife. It is also clear that, unlike her husband, she had a sense of humour. Her books are still worth reading—most of all, perhaps, the one called, engagingly, *The Lady's Country Companion; or How to Enjoy a Country Life Rationally*, which was published in 1845, and did for the outdoor activities of the inexperienced mistress of a Victorian household what Mrs. Beeton's great book did for her indoor economy.

Well may Loudon have said of his wife that he had from her mind ample encouragement and support, adding, truly one hopes, in spite of the pressure of time, that her person was to him a continual delight. One does not imagine her as beautiful, but I think one may suppose that, on the whole, Jane Loudon had a happy life. She certainly deserved it.

CHAPTER II

LOUDON AND ENGLISH GARDENING

Two distinct lines, with not much connexion between them, run through eighteenth-century gardening theory and practice. One of these derived from architecture and developed under the influence of Italian landscape paintings, admired and collected by every English Gentleman on the Grand Tour, into what came to be known as Landscape Gardening—a term invented by Repton for what had long been done by great architects like Vanbrugh and lesser architects like Kent; to say nothing of such poets as Pope and Shenstone. These men and the nobility and gentry whose country estates were the broad canvases on which they worked, cared only for pictorial effects and for romantic and picturesque detail. They discriminated subtly between the sublime and the beautiful, between the grand and the awful, between melancholy and gloom. They read Burke and Lord Kames. "Gardening," said Lord Kames, "beside the emotions of beauty from regularity, order, proportion,

colour, and utility, can raise emotions of grandeur, of
sweetness, of gaiety, of melancholy, of wildness, and even
of surprise and wonder." Indeed, he says, it possesses one
advantage: "never to be equalled in any other art: in
various scenes it can raise successively all the different
emotions above-mentioned".

Side by side with this spectacular landscape art there
was growing up a partly aesthetic, partly scientific,
interest in the new and curious plants which began to
be introduced in large numbers, especially from America.
It has been reckoned that when the Royal Society was
founded after the Restoration there were probably less
than a thousand different kinds of exotic plants grown in
England. Within a century and a half there were more
than six thousand. These were mostly grown in what
were called Botanic Gardens, descendants of the old
apothecaries herb-gardens, at Lambeth, Chelsea, Oxford,
and elsewhere, and such places as the Royal Garden at
Kew, where the possibilities were greatly increased as
the management of greenhouses and hot-houses, invented
towards the end of the seventeenth century, became
better understood.

Independent of this "botanic garden" culture, but in
the end coalescing with it and contributing very much to
the final gardening effect, were the Florists' Clubs which
arose and spread among the artisan population. These
florists' clubs and societies began in East Anglia with the
French and Flemish weavers. They encouraged the
competitive cultivation and improvement of a few species
—tulips, pinks, pansies, auriculas—that showed an uncommon tendency to vary; and by the beginning of the
nineteenth century the enthusiasm for these "florists'"
flowers was intense throughout all the industrial North
and Midlands.

Flower fancying, together with bird fancying and

pigeon fancying—quite different fancy departments—in those days took the place that in ours is taken by football pools, greyhound racing, and the cinema. A writer in one of the many gardening journals that, following Loudon's lead, had sprung up by the 'forties and of which the *Gardener's Chronicle* is the one survivor, describes these clubs as being then past their prime. Their eclipse was a result of the growing demand for house-space and the consequent decrease, ending in the complete elimination, of garden space in all the manufacturing districts of England.

In vain was the country warned that "unless something be done to provide the mechanic with the means of indulging the practice of Floriculture, he will have recourse to the public-house and the skittle-ground, for less-healthy ammusements". Loudon himself, writing in 1829, comments with a hint of Scotch asperity on the Lancashire weavers, among whom it was "no uncommon thing for a working man who earns, perhaps, from 18s. to 30s. per week, to give two guineas for a new variety of auricula, with a view to crossing it with some other and raising seedlings of new properties". Indeed, so all-excluding was the enthusiasm that, as it was said, every cultivator thought more of his flowers than of himself; and some were much more anxious about their gardens than about their wives and children. There were authentic cases of young enthusiasts dying of cold through placing their blankets as a guard against frost over their tulip-beds.

We owe much to these descendants of the displaced persons who fled to our shores from persecution in an age almost as ruthless as our own. They formed in their communities a sort of urban peasantry amongst which a folk art could still flourish. And the florists' flowers may be looked on as the last contribution of the working class

to the common culture—the companions in this respect of
the old Border Ballad and the yet older fairy tale.

It is true that, as with pigeon fancying which produced such freaks as the Tumbler and the Pouter, so it
was also with flower fancying. "The rules for judging of
the beauty or merits of a variety are wholly artificial, and
founded on an imaginary form far removed from ordinary
nature," complained Loudon. And to the later back-
to-nature gardeners this artificiality was, of course,
anathema. One may note, however, that neither William
Robinson nor Gertrude Jekyll dared attack the ancient
and royal rose, symbolic, heraldic, almost magical, but
above all things, highly artificial. Though the rose was
never counted, properly, among the florists' flowers, yet
some of the forms they toiled so patiently to create—
pinks and auriculas and tulips—that are now lost to us
through a too-fanatical condemnation, were hardly less
lovely than the rose itself.

Anyhow, whether one approves of florists' flowers or
not, it was all to the good that, near the turn of the
century, interest in plants was increasing everywhere
among all classes. The London Horticultural Society,
later to become the Royal Horticultural Society, was
founded in 1803, to be followed by many similar societies
up and down the country. To supply the growing demand
for plants, Nursery Gardens sprang up on all sides—
some of which, such as that started by Thomas Rivers at
Sawbridgeworth, or Sutton's great establishment at
Reading, are still with us. At the same time, the landscaping of country-house parks and domains was in the
hands of perhaps its most distinguished practitioner,
Humphry Repton—a man whose genius developed under
the criticism of Sir Uvedale Price, who was in his turn
an enthusiast and amateur of importance.

This was roughly the condition of gardening in

England when Loudon left Edinburgh for London. All its aspects were, for a brief time, in a splendid equilibrium. Francis Bacon, as his great Essay shows, was equally interested in formal or architectural, and in floral gardening. But he had neither the time nor the talents to become a practical gardener. All through the next centuries the two horticultural trends were for the most part separate. Capability Brown cared little or nothing about flowers; and Repton, writing in the dawn of the nineteenth century, could still say of the flower garden that it was only "a sort of episode to the general and magnificent scenery". On the other hand, Philip Miller and the quarrelsome "Sir" John Hill found their main pre-occupation in flowers rather than in tree-belts and canals. Loudon was the first—and almost the last—gardener of importance to be an equal master of the two arts, of landscape gardening and of floriculture. As a further grace, he also mastered the science of the kitchen garden and the orchard.

Landscape gardening Loudon defined, a little pedantically, as "the art of arranging the different parts which compose the external scenery of a country residence, so as to produce the different beauties and conveniences of which that scene of domestic life is susceptible". The passage is hardly fair to his prose style in general, but the precept does seem to have more or less corresponded with his practice. It was characteristic of Loudon, the friend of the Utilitarian, Bentham, to introduce the word "conveniences". He quotes with approval the Reverend Archibald Alison's opinion that it was the landscape gardener's privilege to "create a scenery more pure, more harmonious, and more expressive, than any that is to be found in nature herself".

Yet he rejected the extravagances of the Picturesque school, of which Sir Uvedale Price was the most eloquent ornament. "In short," said Loudon, who was himself a landscape painter, "no comparison between the powers of landscape-painting and those of landscape-gardening can be instituted, that will not evince the superior powers of the former." The gardener "may, and ought, to aim at the highest degree of beauty, which his own imagination, the genius of the place, and the views of the owner, will admit of; but let him not proceed with, or hold out to the world, mistaken views of what his art can and cannot perform".

Among the aspects of beauty, Loudon certainly included the beauty of function or, as he would have said, of convenience:

> "A very common error, since the introduction of the modern style, has been to suppose that picturesque beauty is the only beauty to be aimed at in laying out grounds; but so far from this being the case, it will often happen that the alterations required for the purposes of convenience and character, will lessen that beauty, whilst it increases that of dignity, refinement, and appropriation to man."

And he confirms his view by an example drawn from Repton.

Yet that Loudon was a man of genuine sensibility can be seen from his detailed analysis of an actual landscape, with suggestions for its treatment by the gardener in various ways to produce various effects:

> "As another example of picturesque, and poetic, or sentimental expression, imagine the cattle and sheep removed, the surface of the ground covered by smoothly mown turf, and the luxuriant branches of some of the foreground trees nearly reclining on the ground. The first impression would be that of beautiful

or *elegant* picturesque; the next that of stillness, and consecration to man—stillness, as being without animals or moving objects; and consecration to man, from the mown surface, greatly heightened by the circumstance of the branches of the trees reclining on the ground, which never can happen where sheep or cattle are admitted, and which forms the leading visible distinction between a group of trees in a park, and a group on a mown lawn. It is not from the smoothness of the turf, or any particular mixture of light and shade in the reclining branches, that this expression is produced, but from reflecting on the cause of this appearance."

The whole business implied a sophisticated and educated leisure. In the actual landscape, as Loudon described it, was "a high wall forming the angle of a ruined building", and in the total effect of the scene this building made its emotional contribution:

"The general expression of melancholy and grandeur remains to be accounted for. For this purpose, let the building be the ruins of an ancient castle, whose lofty quadrangular form may be readily imagined from the walls we mentioned as composing a part of the scenery. The character of grandeur, then, is not in this instance communicated to the picture by the picturesque effect of the walls, which have no variety of form, light, or shade, in themselves, but to the mental associations to which they give rise in a cultivated mind."

The modern distinction between the "formal" and the "literary" elements of a picture was obviously a commonplace in Loudon's day.

But this intimate, intricate, introspective, art of

Landscape Gardening was already entering into its decadence. Its greatest effort, its extravagant climax, occurred at Alton Towers, the Staffordshire property of the fifteenth Earl of Shrewsbury. This quite incredible place is now a public park and, as it still exists, was photographed and described for the *Architectural Review* of May 1940 by my friend, Reginald Ross Williamson. Unless one has been there, Mr. Ross Williamson's superb illustrations will hardly be believed.

Loudon, who was consulted by Lord Shrewsbury, though his advice was rejected, gives six pages of print and picture to the gardens (rather inappropriately) in his *Encyclopaedia of Cottage, Farm, and Villa Architecture*:

> "We visited Alton Towers," he says, "in 1826, and again in 1831. On the former occasion we arrived at the house, from Uttoxeter, in the month of October, and on the latter, from Cheadle, in July. By the road leading from Uttoxeter, we came unexpectedly close to the house, and near the head of the north side of the valley, which contains the chief wonders of the place. The first objects that met our eye were, the Gothic bridge and the embankment leading to it, with a huge imitation of Stonehenge beyond and a pond above the level of the bridge alongside it, backed by a mass of castellated stabling."

This imitation of Stonehenge, by the way, was an improvement on the original by the addition of a second range of trilithons superimposed upon the first—as can be seen in Loudon's engraving and in one of Mr. Ross Williamson's illustrations. Loudon continues:

> "Farther along the side of the valley, to the left of the bridge, is a range of architectural conservatories, with seven elegant glass domes, designed by Mr.

Abraham, richly gilt. Farther on still to the left, and placed on a high and bold naked rock, is a lofty Gothic tower or temple, on what is called Thomson's rock, also designed by Mr. Abraham, consisting of several tiers of balconies, round a central staircase and rooms" (Loudon's prose is getting pardonably breathless) "the exterior ornaments numerous, and resplendent with gilding. Near the base of the rock is a corkscrew fountain of a peculiar description, which is amply supplied from an adjoining pond. Behind, above, and beyond the range of conservatories, are two lakes; and beyond them is another conservatory, curiously ornamented: below the main range of conservatories are a paved terrace walk with a Grecian temple at one end, and a second terrace containing a second range of conservatories. The remainder of the valley, to the bottom, and on the opposite side, displays such a labyrinth of terraces, curious architectural walls, trelliswork arbours, vases, statues, stone stairs, wooden stairs, turf stairs, pavements, gravel and grass walks, ornamental buildings, bridges, porticoes, temples, pagodas, gates, iron railings, parterres, jets, ponds, streams, seats, fountains, caves . . ."

Loudon continues for several lines with his list, ending with "entire dead trees". He goes on:

"There is one stair of 100 steps, a cottage for a blind harper as large as a farm house; and an imitation cottage roof, formed by sticking dormer windows, and two chimneys, accompanied by patches of heath to imitate thatch, on the sloping surface of a large grey mass of solid rocks. This seen at a distance, protruding from a steep bank of wood, bore naturally some resemblance to the roof of a cottage grey with lichens; and the chimney-tops and windows were added to complete the idea. As the sandstone rock protrudes from the sides of the valley in immense masses, abundant use has been made of it to form caves, grottoes, caverns and covered seats; it has even been carved into figures; in one place we have Indian temples excavated in it, covered with hiero-glyphics; and in another, a projecting rock is formed as a huge serpent, with a spear-shaped iron tongue and glass eyes.

"There is a rustic prospect-tower over an Indian temple, cut out of solid rock, on the highest point of the north bank; and in the lowest part of the valley there are the foundations and two storeys (executed before the death of the late earl) of an octagon pagoda. This pagoda was intended to be eighty feet high. It is placed on an island in the centre of a small pond, and was to have been approached by a Chinese bridge richly ornamented. The diameter of the base of the pagoda is forty feet, and there were to have been six storeys, the lower one of stone, the others of cast iron. From the angles were to have been suspended forty highly enriched Chinese lamps . . . a column of water was also to have been projected from the terminating ornament."

This pagoda figures among the illustrations to Mr. Ross Williamson's article, and must have been completed in a somewhat abbreviated form after Loudon wrote. That, with some omissions, is an account of Alton Towers as it was approached from Uttoxeter.

Loudon also describes it in the approach from Cheadle. But, though the details are different, to the mind of the reader they add little to the stunning effect of what has already been recounted. Loudon concludes judicially:

"The Scenery of the Valley of Alton Towers is
not here presented as a model for imitation: on
the contrary, we consider the greater part of it in
excessively bad taste, or rather, perhaps, as the
work of a morbid imagination joined to the command
of unlimited resources. Still, however, there are many
excellent things in it, and both the good and the
bad well deserve the attentive study of the young
Architect."

The house itself was largely the work of the great Pugin
who, as Mr. Ross Williamson mentions in his article,
had met the Earl of Shrewsbury in a Wardour Street
furniture shop. Its splendour matched the splendour of
the gardens.

In Alton Towers, even Loudon must have seen the
beginning of the end. What he also saw as he looked
elsewhere around him was the rising of a new class of
garden patrons—the inhabitants of suburban and sub-
suburban Villas. He remarked that

"the kitchen and flower gardens of places of this sort
are generally good, and well furnished with hot-
houses; the shrubbery also is carefully laid out, and
planted with choice shrubs and trees; and as the
proprietor is generally an opulent commercial man,
he is liberal in his annual expenditure. The gardeners
at such places are generally well paid, no limits put
to the dung, implements, structures, or assistance they
may want, and left more entirely to their own discretion than those in the service of country gentlemen."

Your opulent commercial man would not, you might be
sure, display a morbid imagination. His opulence would
ensure a sufficiency of dung; but his being commercial

would prevent extravagance—such as Lord Shrewsbury's casual strewing of a million pounds in the Valley of Alton Towers.

It was to these Villa gardens of from ten to a hundred acres—the word "Villa" had an ampler connotation in those days than in ours—that Loudon for the most part applied himself. The self-made men, their owners, doubtless relied on his taste, and gave him, as later they would give their gardener, a free hand. They were ignorant, but they had no pretensions. They wanted a place that would raise them the least bit in the eyes of their equals, and, given this, Loudon could do what he liked with their grounds. Whereas he found, to his irritation, that he could do nothing with his Bayswater neighbour, the Comte de Vande. The Comte had a garden of but two acres which Loudon found remarkable for its botanical collection, its rose garden, and its general neatness. Yet, criticise as he would, he could not get its aristocratic owner to see that the main walk should not end as a *cul de sac*, that its borders, however interesting their contents, were ill proportioned, and that its boundary fence was paltry. So he turned, regretfully it may be, from the men flung out by the French Revolution to the men flung up by the Industrial Revolution. It is certainly for them more than anyone else that his *Encyclopaedia of Gardening* was written.

And they relied on his *Encyclopaedia*—as their wives came to rely on the *Household Management* of Mrs. Beeton. Both books conveyed, if rightly read, some of the subtleties of what Loudon called the "taste and *ton* of good society". Perhaps it was better to buy two copies of each book—one for the drawing-room or the study, the other for the kitchen or the gardener's lodge. Much of Loudon's book, at any rate, is directed at the working gardener himself.

"With respect to the habits of the family," he is told, "it is not only the duty of the gardener to grow those vegetables, fruits, and flowers, of which the members consume most, or of which they are fondest; but he must also look for other habits of enjoyment; as whether they are fond of walking in the garden, and at what times and places, so as to have everything in the condition and order best adapted for those purposes. Some delight in smells, and for such, the most odoriferous plants should be distributed along the walks; others in sounds, and for these, the trees and plants which produce the fruits preferred by singing birds should be planted . . . Other devices for exciting and keeping alive interest will readily occur to the reflecting gardener."

Loudon, one feels, must have been reading the *Arabian Nights*. But, in fact, he had more probably been either visiting or corresponding with his friend, Charles Waterton, the eccentric Squire of Walton in Yorkshire, and author of the well-known *Wanderings in South America*. In one of his Essays, Waterton remarks:

"Were I asked my opinion of a highly cultivated English flower-garden, I should say that it is the loveliest sight in rural nature; and, moreover, that if it afforded me an opportunity of listening to birds, I should pronounce it little short of absolute perfection. But, in general, the charming melody of birds is of rare occurrence in the modern flower-garden; and I fear that any observations which I may make on this head will not have sufficient weight with them to attract attention to it on the part of the horticulturists."

On another occasion, addressing Loudon direct, he begged him to banish cats from his garden. "You must absolutely chase them away for good and all, otherwise there will be no peace for your birds."

In any case, gardeners "left to their own discretion" had, in Loudon's view, fairly heavy responsibilities. He goes on:

> "Some, in walking, may prefer not being seen by workmen, or at least not meeting them in the paths on which they enjoy this mode of recreation; others may take delight in seeing work going forward, and even in asking questions."

And then there were the sick to be considered:

> "In all families there are invalids at some time or other, and a great object is to render the garden an alleviation to their sufferings. Some, afflicted in the lower extremities, can only walk on grass walks; others, from asthma, may not be able to stoop to smell or gather a rose or a gooseberry; others may require to be carried round the hot-houses in a chair, or wheeled along the walks reclining on a couch, and covered with a glass case. Grass-walks, standard roses, and elevated pots of plants are obvious luxuries for such persons. A sick horticulturist" (he says—and here he was speaking from all-too-severe and all-too-frequent experience), "a sick horticulturist, confined to his chamber, may derive some enjoyment from having pots of plants brought before him for a few minutes, to show him their progress. When life is under the pressure of disease, any object or measure which can divert the attention for a moment affords relief."

And besides the sick, there was another class to which Loudon also belonged:

"Easy turnings in walks are also a great luxury to studious persons, who think as they walk. For this reason, an author, if he can afford any other garden than a pot of mint, should surround this plot with an oval path, that he may walk on without end, and without any sensible change in the position of his body."

Having got into this vein, Loudon addresses the philosopher over the head of the head-gardener as of his commercial master:

"To be condemned to pass an eternity in a pleasure-ground, would be perhaps as dull as to pass it in a conventicle. Man is a social being, and never can reject the habits, to which this part of his nature gives rise, with impunity. To be happy he must see and be seen: it is the operation of this principle that has rendered the most beautiful seats of the country *show-places*; which leads the citizen to place his box or lodge, and the artisan or labourer his cottage or cabin by the roadside; and which, in short, impels the humblest individual to court applause by making his powers, either of purse or mind, known to those around him. A gardener, therefore, must attend to these general principles of our nature as well as he can."

But as Mrs. Beeton laid down the duties not only of the upper servants but also of the kitchen-maids, so also Loudon has suggestions for the under-gardener and the labourer.

Having made up his mind how many under-gardeners and garden labourers he required, the next thing the opulent commercial man was expected to do was "to fix on the hours of labor and of rest, the amount of wages, and regulations as to board. The hours of labor ought to be at least one hour per day less than those for common laborers (who require no mind), in order to allow time for studying the science of the art to be practised. The amount of fines should also be fixed on at the same time: as for absence at the hours of going to labor; for defects of duty, as putting by a tool without cleaning it, being found without a knife or apron, or not knowing the name of a plant."

Were these fines often or ever imposed? one wonders. That Loudon should have suggested them shows the high opinion he had of his profession in all its departments, and the high standard he called for even in its humbler followers.

"In leaving off working at any job, leave your work and tools in an orderly manner," he tells them. "Are you hoeing between rows, do not throw down your hoe blade upwards, or across the rows, and run off the nearest way to the walk the moment the breakfast or dinner hour strikes. Lay your implement down parallel to the rows, with its face or blade to the ground; then march regularly down one row to the alley, and along the alley to the path. Never drop your tools and leave off work before the hour has well done striking; and above all, never run on an occasion of this kind; it argues a gross brutalised selfishness, highly offensive to well-regulated minds."

Heavens, had Loudon been reading Lord Chesterfield? —"Among other things, let me caution you against ever being in a hurry; a man of sense may be in haste, but he is never in a hurry . . . Walking fast in the street is a sign of vulgarity." But Chesterfield had his awkward son in view. Loudon was pointing to a hard furrow for men who had been hoeing, perhaps for hours, without breakfast. And then "Finally" (Loudon at the end of his longish lecture admonishes the aspiring gardener), "finally, attend to personal habits and to cleanliness. Never perform any operation without gloves on your hands that you can do with gloves on."

In those days even the shilling-a-day female labourer, who must have needed very little mind in searching for insects and worms on Saturday, searching for snails and slugs on Monday, weeding turnips on Tuesday, gathering green gooseberries for wine on Wednesday and Thursday, and weeding the walks on Friday—as she did at Aubrey Hall between June 8th and 15th of the year 1823—even she, A. Teisel, was supplied with gloves, the forefingers and thumbs of which were armed with sharp wedge-shaped thimbles of steel. From the "Remarks" at the end of that week's "Occupation Sheet" one learns that there were only two days' sunshine in the seven, that the Russian Ambassador called on Tuesday, and that Teisel wished her weeding-gloves repointed. Also that she was much pleased with the Amazon working-dress given her by my Lady Almeria. However it may be about "Amazon working-dresses", it is surprising that those gloves with steel finger-nails should have gone out of fashion—they must have been deadly to slugs and insects, and invaluable for weeding.

From Loudon's books one gets a view of life as it was lived more than a hundred years ago. It is not the same view one gets from the novels of Jane Austen or the poems of Crabbe, but it is fully as authentic and in some ways more curious. In his *Self-Instruction for Young Gardeners* he reproduces a page from the "Kitchen-Book" kept by Mr. Barnes, head-gardener at Bicton, the seat of the Right Honourable Lady Rolle. It is the "Vegetable, Fruit, and Flower List for the Week ending Saturday, September 25th, 1842". During that one week, forty different sorts of culinary vegetable were sent in, besides another eight sorts for raw salad, and yet another seven for picklings; there were also twelve different sorts of cooking fruit, and orange flowers and magnolia flowers for preserving; then there were twenty different sorts of table-fruit, including three kinds of pine-apple. The flowers were not specified in such detail, but there were two baskets of cut flowers, eight dozen dahlias, four dozen magnolia flowers, and forty plants for baskets in the front hall. Not everything was eaten every day, of course. There was only one dish of mushrooms, and the *Cycas revoluta* fruit was eaten but twice; on the other hand, they had a single melon on four days, and on the Monday they seem to have got through no less than ten. "It will be observed," says Loudon, "that the gardens at Bicton are on a very large scale; and that consequently comparatively few gardens will need so extensive a Kitchen-Book."

All the same, even if there were not many gardens on quite that scale, those were the great days of domestic gardening. Income-tax was about twopence in the pound. Wages might, for a foreman gardener, be as much as twenty-five shillings a week—Mr. Barnes of Bicton, of course, got more—but for the most part they would be more like fifteen or sixteen shillings. Trade was good, and plants were plenty. Plants, indeed, were simply pouring in from the ends of the earth. Robert Fortune was collecting for the Horticultural Society and the East India Company in China; the unlucky David Douglas, killed at thirty-six by a wild bull, was collecting, also for the Horticultural Society, in temperate North America; and there were many others, like the Icelandic scholar, William Herbert, Dean of Manchester, who collected assiduously and acutely on their travels in Europe, North Africa, and the near East.

It was the age of the Glasshouse: of anything from Paxton's 300-foot erections, down which one looked as into a primaeval forest of the Brazils, at Chatsworth, to the elegant Wardian Case with its arrangement of an orchid and a few ferns on the drawing-room table. A rough reckoning of the new plant species and varieties first made known in England in 1845—a fair sample year —shows that of 238 plants only some 34 or 35 were hardy, All the rest, including 55 new orchids, were greenhouse, conservatory, or stove plants. At the time the disproportion seemed even greater, for several plants, such as *Calandrinia umbellata* and *Iris stylosa*, introduced by Dean Herbert, were then supposed to be tender.

This enormous preponderance of hot-house exotics was partly the creator of and partly the response to a demand. With Lord Macartney's embassy to the Emperor of China in 1793 the great flow of plants from the Orient had begun, and these being mostly lowland plants, needed glasshouses for their culture in England. Then, as the use of glass with artificial heating became better understood, nurserymen like Veitch of Chelsea sent their own collectors to Asia and to tropical America. So was set up a sort of snowball emphasis between tender tropical plants and ever more elaborate greenhouses.

Loudon's second book, published in 1805, was *A Short Treatise on Some Improvements Lately Made in Hothouses*. He himself, if he did not invent, was the first to popularise glasshouses with iron-framed roofs on a curvilinear principle, and all his life he kept up his interest in this branch of gardening. By the time his *Encyclopaedia* was published the successful culture of tropical and sub-tropical plants had become a complex and highly technical art. Amateurs classed these plants in four categories: first there were those that could be grown in an ordinary "cold" greenhouse without additional heat; next, those that were suitable for the conservatory which would be slightly heated in winter; then those which required what was called the "dry stove", where the July temperature must be kept at from seventy to eighty-five degrees by day and from sixty to seventy by night; and finally there was the orchid-house or "bark stove" whose temperature must never fall below seventy, and was held at something over ninety on a summer day. In this last, the pots containing the plants were plunged in a bed of fermenting bark for additional heat.

Loudon, who had a true visionary's imagination—it had been the earliest bond between himself and his wife —let himself go over the possibilities of glasshouses:

"Indeed," he says, "there is hardly any limit to the extent to which this sort of light roof might be carried; several acres, even a whole country residence, where the extent was moderate, might be covered in this way, by the use of hollow cast-iron columns as props, which might serve also as conduits for the water which fell on the roof. Internal showers might be produced in Loddiges' manner [Messrs. Loddiges were a firm of nurserymen of Hackney]; or the roof might be of the polyprosophic kind, and opened at pleasure to admit the natural rain. Any required temperature might be kept up by the use of concealed tubes of steam, and regulated by the apparatus of Kewley [inventor of a regulating thermometer called the 'automaton gardener']. Ventilation also would be effected by the same machine. . . . Such a roof might be raised to the height of a hundred or a

hundred and fifty feet from the ground, to admit of
the tallest oriental trees, and the undisturbed flight
of appropriate birds among their branches. A variety
of oriental birds and monkeys, and other animals,
might be introduced; and in ponds, a stream made
to run by machinery, and also in salt lakes, fishes,
polypi, corals, and other productions of fresh or sea
water might be kept."

In other words, add together the Parrot House at the Zoo,
the Fern House at Kew, and the Brighton Aquarium, and
multiply the sum by ten—then go and live in it.

At the opposite end of the scale, the "Wardian Case"
provided an interest which might, one feels in these days
of flats, very well be revived. The Case was invented, or
rather its principle was accidentally discovered, by
Nathaniel Ward, who in 1829 put a moth-chrysalis
in a bottle with some damp earth, corked it up and forgot
about it. When he next saw his bottle it contained a
flourishing plant which had grown from a seed in the
wet soil, and had continued alive and well in closely
corked confinement. The principle was investigated by
scientists such as Faraday who himself lectured on it,
and very soon Wardian Cases were being made com-
mercially and were to be found, supporting in their un-
changing atmospheres a variety of charming exotics, on
the window-table of every lady's boudoir. The Case was
also adapted to the large-scale transport of tropical plants,
and was of great use to collectors. But the Wardian Case
was too trivial, too insignificant a structure, for Loudon's
notice. What he wanted was something that "might form
an appropriate appendage to a palace in the oriental
style"—and he gives a drawing of the appendage with
the palace in the background.

It was the growing vogue for hot-house plants that

led to the great bedding and carpet-bedding craze of the 'forties, 'fifties, and 'sixties. This involved the summer planting-out, generally in their pots, of greenhouse or other tender shrubs and herbaceous plants. The idea was as old, in England, as Sir William Chambers's *Dissertations on Oriental Gardening* of 1774.

> "In their large plantations," Chambers says, speaking of the Chinese, "the flowers generally grow in the natural ground; but in flower-gardens, and all other parts that are highly kept, they are in pots, buried in the ground, which, as fast as the bloom goes off, are removed, and others are brought to supply their places; so that there is a constant succession for almost every month in the year; and the flowers are never seen but in the height of their beauty."

However, the eighteenth century, except for an odd gardener like the poet William Mason, was not much interested in floral effects. And even when Loudon was writing in 1822, bedding-out was practised to only a trifling extent—he refers to it in no detail and in the smallest print.

Joseph Paxton was among the first to grasp the great possibilities of the Chinese idea, and it was from Chatsworth and one or two other great gardens that bedding-out spread to the conquest of England. But that conquest was hardly complete in Loudon's time.

For him, there were two main methods of growing flowers out of doors. The first was the "mingled flower-garden, or border". This was by far the most common. It differed from our usual herbaceous borders in that it was the accepted rule for flowers in borders always to be planted in rows. "Every approach to irregularity and a wild, confused, crowded, or natural-like appearance

must be avoided in gardens avowedly artificial". Apart
from regimental rows, the important thing was colour-
grouping, and on this Loudon had original theories. He
thought that

> "flower-gardens looked best when the flowers were so
> arranged as to have a compound colour next the
> simple one which was not contained in it. Thus, as
> there are only three simple colours, blue, red, and
> yellow, he advises that purple flowers, which are
> composed of blue and red, should have yellow next
> them; that orange flowers, which are composed of
> red and yellow, should be contrasted with blue; and
> that green flowers, which are composed of blue and
> yellow, should be relieved by red."

These ingenious proposals, which remind one of the
colour-theorising of the Dorset poet, William Barnes,
were based, in Loudon's case, on the esoteric principle
that three parts are required to make a perfect whole;
and he compared the three primitive colours with the
common chord in music. However that may be, his
colour schemes for the mingled flower-garden were
probably effective.

The other kind of garden that Loudon considered
important was the

> "*select flower-garden*, in which the object is limited to the
> cultivation of particular kinds of plants; as, florist's
> flowers, American plants, annuals, bulbs, etc. Some-
> times two or more classes are included in one garden,
> as bulbs and annuals; but in general, the best effect is
> produced by limiting the object to one class only."

Then there was the interesting garden of "Frame
Exotics". Frame exotics were supposed to be rather

hardier than most greenhouse plants, and were kept in
frames or pits which could be covered with mats during
hard frosts. Loudon thought that few scenes were more
charming in the spring-time than

> "a small oblong flower-garden, surrounded by a
> holly-hedge enriched with many spikes of coral
> berries: within the hedge a sloping frame-border all
> round; on the north side, containing frame exotics;
> on the west, early flowering bulbs; on the east, choice
> auriculas; and on the south side (the border facing
> north) a collection of alpines. The middle of the
> garden might be laid out in beds of florist's flowers."

It was obviously from such a garden as this that, by a
single step, full-fledged bedding-out might have derived.

Florist's flowers Loudon deals with separately in some
detail. They had long been cultivated, and were widely
popular in the early eighteenth century, when Thomson
was writing *The Seasons*:

> Anemones; auriculas, enriched
> With shining meal o'er all their velvet leaves;
> And full ranunculus of glowing red.
> Then comes the tulip-race, where beauty plays
> Her idle freaks: from family diffused
> To family, as flies the father-dust,
> The varied colours run; and, while they break
> On the charmed eye, the exulting Florist marks
> With secret pride the wonders of his hand.

And Loudon hoped to induce the wealthier classes to take
them up, but in fact they did not make very much head-
way among the well-to-do until after Loudon's death.

One other branch of gardening interested Loudon—
interested him perhaps more than any other. This was

the growing of ornamental trees. His first book was called *Observations on the Formation and Management of Useful and Ornamental Plantations*. He was a lover of trees:

> "In travelling through a naked country, a whole unvaried horizon is comprehended by the eye at a single glance; its surface is totally destitute of intricacy to excite curiosity and fix attention: and both the eye and the mind are kept in a state of perpetual weariness and fatigue. But in a wooded country the scene is continually changing; the trees form a varied boundary to every thing around, and enter into numberless and pleasing combinations with all other objects; the eye is relieved without distraction, and the mind fully engaged without fatigue. If we examine even a tree by itself, the intricate formation and disposition of its boughs, sprays, and leaves, its varied form, beautiful tints, and diversity of light and shade, make it far surpass every other object; and, notwithstanding this multiplicity of parts, its general effect is simple and grand."

Loudon had been journeying between London and Perth and back, and had been bored by the unwooded Midlands; yet surely, as passed through in a mail coach no less than in a railway train or a motor-bus, forest scenery is not at its best?—one wants to walk or perhaps ride in Savernake Forest

> When autumn first, from the long avenue,
> That lifts its arching height of ancient shade,
> Steals here and there a leaf!

After his piece of rather special pleading, Loudon refers to various uses of timber, and then goes on:

"But, independently of the beauty and profit of wood, the pleasure attending the formation and management of plantations will be a considerable recommendation to every virtuous mind. We look upon our young trees as our offspring; and nothing can possibly be more satisfying than to see them grow and prosper under our care and attention; nothing more interesting than to examine their progress, and mark their several peculiarities. As they advance to perfection, we foresee their ultimate beauty; and the consideration that we have reared them raises a most agreeable train of sensations in our minds; so innocent and rational, that they may justly rank with the most exquisite of human gratifications."

Nowadays, when no one expects his children, much less his grand-children, to live in the place that he lives in, having no longer a simple solid faith in endless futures vista'd down the years, we tend to leave our tree-planting to the Forestry Department, and confine ourselves to flowering shrubs. It seems a pity to miss what our great-grandfathers found to be one of the most exquisite of human gratifications.

A hundred years ago, things were so settled, security was so broadening down from precedent to precedent whilst securities accumulated, that it was common practice to plant a collection of specimen trees, an *Arboretum*; or, less ambitiously, a *Pinetum* of conifers—the sort of thing that William Howitt, the Quaker, describes in the garden of his friend the great Earl of Shaftesbury at Richmond in 1845:

"A pleasanter lawn and shrubberies are rarely to be seen; the turf, old and mossy, speaks of long duration and great care; the trees, dispersed beauti-

E

fully upon it, are of the finest growth and of the greatest beauty.

"In no part of England are there so many foreign trees as in the grounds of gentlemen's villas near London; in many of them the cedars of Lebanon are of a growth and majesty which probably Lebanon itself cannot now show. In these grounds are some fine specimens, and one of especial and surpassing loveliness; it is the *pinus picea*, or silver cedar. The growth is broad, like that of the cedar of Lebanon, though its boughs do not throw themselves out in that exact horizontal direction that those of the cedar of Lebanon do; they sweep down to the ground in a style of exquisite grace. Heavy, full of life, rich in hue as masses of chased silver, their effect with the young cones sitting birdlike on them resembles that of some tree of heaven, or of some garden of poetic romance.

"Besides this superb tree standing on its ample portion of lawn, there are here the evergreen ilex, hickory, white sassafras, scarlet and Ragland oaks, the tulip tree, the catalpa, the tupelo, the black American ash, etc. The effect of their large growth, their varied hues and foliage, their fine branches sweeping over the soft velvet turf, is charming; for trees display the effects of breeding and culture quite as much as horses, dogs, or men."

Which goes to show that Loudon, who laid out many such small estates near London, was not peculiar in his enthusiasm. Howitt mentions Lord Shaftesbury's mossy and well-cared-for lawn. Moss is not now thought much of in lawns. But though lawn-mowers, invented by a Mr. Budding, were first put on the market in 1831, (Loudon describes them with approval in the *Gardener's*

Magazine), yet it is clear, from Victorian gardening literature, that for very many years the vast areas of English lawn continued to be cut by scythe—which would account for the encouragement of moss.

Loudon also gave a good deal of time to kitchen gardening, on which his instructions and advice were so authoritative that William Robinson, rather than write a book on this not very exciting subject himself, re-edited in 1871 Loudon's volume on *The Culture and Management of the Kitchen, Fruit, and Forcing Garden.* This is, as one would expect, an uncommonly thorough and detailed work, most logically arranged. Loudon was not only a practical gardener, he had also read every book that had been written on gardening during the previous 150 years —though when he found time to do so is a mystery. But mere vegetables appealed only to the Benthamite side of his mind; in dealing with them there was nothing to call his picturesque imagination into play. His worthy book is probably nearly as useful now as it was when he wrote it or when Robinson reissued it.

This is not the place, nor am I the person to discuss Loudon's standing as an architect or as a writer about architecture, except to say that here as elsewhere he obviously touched nothing that he did not master. But leaving that, and his activities as naturalist and painter entirely out of account, John Claudius Loudon was beyond question a great English gardener; and therefore, no less than if he had been a statesman, a soldier, or a poet, one of England's Great Men. Of his contemporaries, only Paxton comes near him, but he was followed by an age in which there were to be many great gardeners.

CHAPTER III

WILLIAM ROBINSON, EXILE OF ERIN

LOUDON, the greatest English gardener of his day, died at the end of 1842. Some four years earlier, on 15 July, 1838, was born perhaps the greatest English gardener of his own or any other day.

As Loudon was a Scotsman, so William Robinson was an Irishman. He was born either in the Queen's County, now marked as Leix on the Irish maps, or in County Dublin, of humble Protestant parentage. Nothing is known of his earliest years. Like Meredith he was reticent if not misleading about his origins—so causing gossip and suspicion of illegitimacy. He was probably given an elementary education at the parish school. It may well have been quite a good education, though inferior to what Loudon, coming from an equivalent social stratum, received in Scotland fifty years earlier.

The first ascertainable fact about Robinson's life is his apprenticeship as garden-boy to the Reverend Sir Hunt Henry Johnson-Walsh of Ballykilcannan, Stradbally.

Sir Hunt Johnson-Walsh was a baronet, a graduate of Dublin University, and Vicar of Stradbally. He was also a large local landowner, and a considerable gardener. At least, he maintained by Irish standards a considerable garden; though it must be remembered that the Irish have never held gardening in their blood and bones as the English have—otherwise the next important step in Robinson's career could, perhaps, hardly have been taken.

Robinson got on well in the garden at Ballykilcannan, rising to be foreman by the time he was twenty-one, and having control over extensive conservatories and hot-houses. All his life he seems, to say the least of it, to have been critical and plain-spoken. In the winter of 1861, when he was twenty-three, he had a sudden and violent disagreement either with the head-gardener or with Sir Hunt himself. What it was all about, its rights and wrongs, are now beyond discovery; but Robinson considered himself ill-treated and took immediate drastic action. It was a period of bitter frost, and that night, without saying a word the Reverend Sir Hunt Johnson-Walsh's trusted foreman-gardener drew out all the fires in the glasshouses and opened every window. By dawn next day the whole collection of tropical plants must have been dead or dying, but by dawn next day the delinquent had arrived in Dublin.

In Dublin, Robinson, feeling, one hopes, very much as though he had shot a fox, made his way to the Royal Botanic Gardens at Glasnevin. There he waited on the Director, a Scotsman, Dr. David Moore, to whom he was already slightly known. Dr. Moore could not have looked with less than horror on the shocking act of the young gardener. But he must also have seen extenuating circumstances; and he must have foreseen the young man's genius. In any case, the upshot of this deplorable escapade was that Robinson went to London where, on Dr. Moore's recommendation, he found employment, with a wage of nine shillings a week, at the Royal Botanic Society's garden in Regent's Park.

The Royal Botanic Society had been founded in 1839 by the then Duke of Norfolk as something of a rival to the Royal Horticultural Society. The first Curator of the Society's garden was Robert Marnock, a well-known landscape gardener of the time. Here again Robinson got on well, and within two years he was appointed foreman of the herbaceous section of the garden. He also attracted the attention and gained the friendship of Marnock, through whom he was elected a Fellow of the Linnean Society—a signal honour for a man in his position. One of his supporters at the election was Charles Darwin, for whose theories and opinions Robinson later conceived a possibly justified but certainly incoherent detestation.

This was whilst he was still at Regent's Park. But the most significant occurrence of those years with the Royal Botanic Society was that Marnock put him in charge of the Society's small garden of English wild flowers. This unique garden had to be kept up and added to from time to time; and Robinson mentions in the preface to the later editions of his *English Flower Garden* how the search for suitable plants led him into the beauty of the woods and lanes and past the lovely cottage gardens of the country round London—a country which in the 'sixties was many miles nearer to Regent's Park than it is now—led him farther afield, too, so that in various plant-collecting expeditions he got to know a wide area from, as he says, the orchid-flecked meadows of Buckinghamshire to the tumbled-down undercliffs on the Essex coast.

Robinson had naturally sharp eyes, and his botanising in the countryside gave him an eye for the natural habit of a plant, from which he "began to get an idea that there was, for gardens even, much beauty in our native flowers and trees, and then came the thought that if there was so much in our own island flora, what might we not look for from the hills and valleys of the countries of the northern and temperate world?"

This idea was a germ which, if it did not grow at once and at a weed's pace—he was inclined in later years to exaggerate its rate of growth—was yet charged with a potent vitality.

It was at about this time also—within a year or so of his coming to London, that the one romantic attachment of Robinson's long life occurred. He met, and perhaps walked out with on his botanical rambles, a young woman to whom he became engaged, but who, being of a mercenary turn, jilted him for a prosperous tradesman. Robinson's heart may not have been broken, but he seems never to have ventured it again.

During these years in London he must have been taking his own education seriously in hand; for, apart from his election to the Linnean Society, when he was barely twenty-nine he left the Botanic Society's garden in order to go as representative of the great nursery-garden firm of Veitch and as Special Horticultural Correspondent of *The Times* to the Paris Exhibition of 1867. For this expedition he learned French from a French *émigré*, his accent becoming so good that, later, a French ancestry was hinted at, and not always denied.

From then on, Robinson never looked back. His articles in *The Times* made him widely known and gave him authority; and on them he based his first book, *Gleanings from French Gardens*, which was followed in 1869 by his *Parks, Promenades, and Gardens of Paris*. From Paris, in the summer of 1868, Robinson visited various gardens and horticultural centres throughout France. In June of the next year he made his first visit to the Alps. He was enchanted with Geneva, "associated as it is with thoughts of Rousseau and the author of the *Prisoner of Chillon*". He became distinctly nervous in the Saas Valley. It had begun to rain.

> "With rapid pace and eyes fixed on the stony footway, on we went, the valley becoming narrower as we progressed, and in some parts dangerous-looking from almost perpendicularly rising hills of loose stone. Presently a little rough weather-beaten cross was passed beside the footway. 'Why a cross here?' said I to the guide. 'That great stone or rock you see, killed, on its way down, a man returning with his marketings up the valley,' he replies. Ten minutes afterwards we came to a group of three more rough wooden crosses. They marked the spot where two women and a man had been buried by an avalanche."

Thereafter, crosses began to occur so thickly "as to remind one of a cemetery", and he began to think that it would be safer to be in a railway collision than in the valley of the Saas. Also the rain turned to snow. But miserable and scared as he was, he could still notice, on the lee side of rocks, the "pretty little yellow *Viola biflora*", and the "beautiful, soft, crimson, white-eyed flowers of *Primula viscosa*". Two days later he crossed the pass of Monte Moro into Italy. He was impressed by his crossing of the Alps, as all other pedestrian travellers have been, from Hannibal to Wordsworth. At the top of the pass

> "a new and magnificent prospect bursts upon us— the white clouds lie in three thin layers along the sides

of Monte Rosa, but permit us to see its crest, while
the great mountains whose snowy heads tower around
it are here seen in all their majesty. On the Swiss side
nothing but snow is seen on peak or in hollow; on
the Italian, a deep valley has wormed its way among
the magnificent mountain peaks, crested with sun-lit
snow and dark crags, and guarded by vast ice rivers
and unscaleable heights. We can gaze into this
valley as easily as one does from a high building into
the street below; and, crouched on the sunny side of a
vertical cliff, to gain a little shelter from the icy
breeze that flowed over the pass, view its quiet signs
of life and green meadows, and above their highest
fringes the vast funereal groves of pines on every
side, guarding as it were, the green valley from the
deathlike wastes of snow above it."

The style is a little self-conscious, and Robinson had
been reading Ruskin, whom he later came to know and
venerate; but he clearly had an observant eye—for a
landscape no less than for a flower. In Italy he visited
the great Lakes, where his opinion of the Borromean
Islands coincided with Loudon's in disparagement—Isola
Bella being too stylised, too formal an artifact for these
ardent naturalists.

One of the results of his Alpine walking-tour was the
publication in 1870 of *Alpine Flowers for English Gardens*.
This, I think, was the first book on Rock Gardening to
be published since James Lothian's *Practical Hints on the
Culture and General Management of Alpine or Rock Plants* of
1845, which, though tentative and wrong-headed in
many ways, seems to have been the pioneer book on its
subject.

In the autumn of 1870 Robinson paid his first visit to
America. He had a strong affinity for the United States,

its people and its plants. The Sierras called forth as much
enthusiasm as the Alps and caused less discomfort:

"To the western slopes of the great chain of the
Sierras one must go to see the noblest trees and the
richest verdure. There every one of thousands of
mountain gorges, and the pleasant and varied flanks
of every vale, and every one of the innumerable hills,
are densely populated with noble pines and glossy
evergreens, like an ocean of huge land waves, over
which the spirit of tree-life has passed, creating giants.
The autumn days I spent among these trees were
among the happiest one could desire."

As always, he was observant—noticing how pretty
were the "old and neglected Box edgings grown into low
hedges" in the garden of George Washington's old home
at Mount Vernon, and gathering seed from the best
forms of phlox and pentstemon. His enthusiastic and life-
long interest in North American plants is, in some ways,
regrettable, for however one may account for or analyse
the fact, it remains a fact that most of these garden
introductions from Canada and the United States lack,
at the least, a certain old-world charm. In this same
year, 1870, was published Robinson's fourth book, *The
Wild Garden, or Our Groves and Shrubberies Made Beautiful.*
In this and in the *Alpine Flowers* he fired his first shots
in his long war against the "bedders-out"—though "shots"
is too sharp a word for the comparative mildness with
which these two delightful little books urged, or rather
pleaded for, the growing of hardy exotics in a natural
manner. The second edition of *The Wild Garden* was so
extensively rewritten as to be, to all intents and purposes,
a different book. Nearly a third of the pages in the first
edition are taken up by an engaging essay on "The Garden

of British Wild Flowers" which was never reprinted and was obviously written whilst the memory of plant-hunting expeditions in the Home Counties was still fresh in his mind. Quotations from Tennyson, Byron, Emerson, Ruskin, and Carlyle show that the thirty-two-year-old gardener and author was getting through a good deal of miscellaneous reading. At this stage, too, his ear was still sensitive to the music of words, and both these volumes of 1870 have a grace of style which his later prose conspicuously lacks.

In the next year, 1871, Robinson, having saved up enough money, founded *The Garden*, a weekly paper that at first barely paid its way. He edited *The Garden* through more than fifty half-yearly volumes. From the beginning it helped to establish and extend the influence he had gained as horticultural correspondent of *The Times*. And by it he also made the acquaintance of his life-long friend and faithful, though ever independent, ally Gertrude Jekyll—a gardener whose impact on the horticultural scene was only a little lighter than his own. "Robinson at Garden Office" is an entry in Miss Jekyll's diary for January 1875. A few years later he and Dean Hole, the great rose grower, visited her at Munstead. From then on, the friendship between Gertrude Jekyll and William Robinson ripened. Had it become more than friendship, what a race of garden giants might have sprung from their union! As it was, Robinson was given a hand in the layout of her famous garden then in the making.

About this time, 1879, Robinson founded a second weekly paper called *Gardening*. It proved to be his financial turning-point. For *Gardening* was a popular illustrated paper. It was written for the prosperous inhabitants of suburban villas—the villa had contracted considerably since Loudon's day—and, unlike *The Garden*, it was an immediate and overwhelming success. Forty years later, when he was at last giving it up as a result of the First World War, he could look back with satisfaction.

"From its birth to the present year" (he wrote, either in December 1918 or January 1919), "it was my happy lot to pilot *Gardening* through fair-weather seas. Started without noise in the Press and without an advertisement, in a few weeks it was a success, and so went on for many years, meeting no enemies and many friends, until the Hun arose in his might to devastate the world."

Well may Robinson have been satisfied. He was forty-one. Eighteen years earlier, he had left Ireland under something of a cloud and penniless. Now he was growing rich. In a short time, with the money his new paper had made for him invested in London house property, he found himself a man of great wealth. It was in the late 'seventies or early 'eighties that he made one of his few commercial and journalistic mistakes. In a fit of pique he started a daily newspaper called *London*. What passing freak of ill-temper led him so to misjudge his vocation I do not know: but that it was indeed a mistake he himself very soon saw, and he almost immediately cut his losses by suspending publication. His losses were not remarkable. *Gardening Illustrated* soon cleared them. And in 1884 he felt himself justified in filling a long-felt want. He bought Gravetye Manor, near East Grinstead in Sussex, and with it more than two hundred acres of good English land.

Gravetye Manor is described in the *Sussex Archaeological Collection* as "an old Elizabethan stone mansion in the parish of West Hoathly, retaining much of its ancient appearance, as when built at the close of the sixteenth century, with its broad mullioned windows and terraced garden". Here Robinson lived for the rest of his long life. For half a century Gravetye was his absorbing passion. It was wife and child and kingdom to him. It was his daily theme. Always and ever he was scheming out alterations and improvements. His old friend and early patron, Robert Marnock, then a man of eighty-four, came down and helped him with the "landscaping". Alfred Parsons, the illustrator of several of his books, helped him with architectural revisions.

One of the first structural alterations that had to be undertaken concerned the heating of the house. Robinson had a fanatical dislike for coal fires. They induced a sort of grumpy irritation whenever he thought of them.

"Such is the vogue of coal," he said, "that even where wood is abundant one may see people crowding round ugly iron grates trying to warm themselves; and there is an idea that you cannot be warmed with wood fires—a stupid mistake arising out of the fact that the good old way of managing wood fires is to a great extent lost."

Even his cooking had to be done over wood.

He found, however, that for some reason logs would not burn in the Gravetye fireplaces. He then remembered, or fancied he did, that wood-burning had survived in France much more generally than it had in England. He therefore sent to Paris for a French *fumiste*, who not only converted, or in some cases reconverted, all the Gravetye coal-grates into open hearths, but also enlarged all the chimneys and introduced elaborate ventilating arrangements for securing correct draughts.

He must have spent a small fortune on his fireplaces and flues, and since in mediaeval days the Manor must have been heated by wood, some of the expense was probably unnecessary; but he got a lot of fun out of it, and he wrote a detailed description of every fireplace in the house:

"The hall, the largest room, is where the people who built the house used to dine with their retainers. It had once a fire hearth of the old sort, but in the course of changes from a merchant's country house to an almost abandoned one, the fireplace was altered and not for the better. When I saw it first it was in the time of the aesthetic craze of Oscar Wilde, and an attempt had been made to improve it. A basket grate was placed in the fireplace flanked by mirrors, with a sunflower painted on each, leaving just room to see one's boots reflected. We got rid of all this and found the old iron plate below a mass of concrete and other rubbish. . . . The fire-back is one from the Louvre of the time of Louis XIII."

One would like to have seen the Oscar Wildeish arrange-ment, but no doubt Robinson's was an improvement—aesthetically and calorically. Whilst all this reconstruc-tion was going on, Robinson lived in the Moat Cottage, one of the smaller houses on his extensive estate.

When it was finished, it was all very sumptuous, and in 1911, by way of memorial to its sumptuousness, he published a folio volume, printed by the Oxford University Press, on hand-made paper, bound in white vellum, tied with green silk ribands, and called *Gravetye Manor, or Twenty Years' Work Round an Old Manor House*. This richly dressed, almost overdressed, book is made up of extracts from Robinson's diary. The entries have a bald artless-ness in curious, not unpleasing, contrast to the medium by which they are presented.

The Diary begins with the making of a tennis-court;

lawn tennis was ten years old and all the rage in 1885. It records how in 1889 he bought Mill Place, an estate adjoining Gravetye, and started farming with a flock of sheep—ninety ewes at £3 15s. to £4 12s. apiece—and a pedigree herd of Sussex cattle. His farming was a financial failure, but for years he kept up his herd of Sussex cattle at a loss because he found "the manner in which the cows, calves, and all group themselves in the fields a constant source of pleasure". In fact, "everything was done," as he says, "with regard to landscape beauty, whether roadside fence, plantation, covert—all was done with that in view". He changed the direction of fences that hid the views of beautiful meadows. He changed the names of the meadows themselves, re-calling them romantically "Birchfalls", "Brookbanks", "Mill Place Mead", "Dean Pasture", and so on, in place of their prosaic and numerical acreage. And then there was the garden. The place had at first been wrongly planted and afterwards long neglected.

"All Welingtonias cut down as being at once ugly and unsuited to the climate," he notes. "Many Daffodils of various kinds were planted in the meadows in November: common English sorts by lower end of lake, Poets on the lawn near the Oaks to the right as one goes down Smugglers Lane, Poets along the streamlet in the Moat meadow, and Tenby Daffodil on the slope of Sweetbriar meadow where it falls to the Water."

And in 1890 he put in 10,000 Calabrian pines—two-year-old trees obtained from France. It was opulent planting.

To start with, he had a number of glasshouses at Gravetye, but he found his gardeners spending too much time in them. "A horrid race this pot and kettle idea of a garden would have led to: men to get chills if their gloves were not aired. I met the difficulty myself by abolishing glass altogether." Was this the real reason and the only one? Or was it partly a dislike of the Paxtonian Crystal Palace methods of gardening which went with so much else that he disliked? And how much of his anti-glasshouse emotion would a psychiatrist put down to that long-ago, unexpiated escapade on the last night at Ballykilcannan—like living in a glasshouse when you want to throw stones? Whatever the cause, simple or complex, Robinson could and did get on very well without conservatories, greenhouses, stoves—the whole early Victorian bag of glass tricks.

In the meantime, if the adorning of Gravetye was his main preoccupation, he had plenty of energy for other lesser occupations: foreign travel, including the Mediterranean and North Africa, where "among the Kabyle villages he passed many vines of great age trailing over very old olive trees in the little orchard fields"; remodelling the gardens at Shrubland Park in Suffolk for Lord de Saumarez, which marked a triumph for his ideas, since Shrublands had long been one of the most famous bedding-out gardens in England. But above all, he was writing.

In the winter of 1883, just before he took possession of his Manor House, he published the first edition of *The English Flower Garden*, the issue of new editions of which kept him continuously and contentedly busy in his spare time for the rest of his life. It was his greatest work—it and the garden at Gravetye. And the book has proved more lasting than the garden.

Gardening and writing were, one might have thought, fairly quiet and peaceful occupations. But Robinson had in him a combative, not to say a quarrelsome, streak. He was hardly well settled into Gravetye than for some

William Robinson on his 90th birthday

reason the villagers began to plague him. They pretended that his property, up to the very walls of his house, was riddled with rights of way. These alleged rights he contested in an embittered law-suit by which at last he greatly reduced their number and entirely closed all those that were supposed to cross the seven acres immediately surrounding the Manor House. The local population seems to have been provoking; but Robinson was not conciliatory, and he spoke and wrote as if all rights of way everywhere were an intolerable evil—forgetting his long plant-collecting rambles of twenty years gone by.

His writing, too, as his prestige increased, became markedly more uncompromising. Against Kew and its gentle director, Sir Joseph Hooker, he carried on an entirely one-sided war because Kew maintained a certain amount of bedding-out; and also because it persisted, despite all Robinson's protests, in labelling plants with Latin names and not with English. On this question of plant-names he had a bee in his bonnet which he had caught from Ruskin and which ultimately got enmeshed in the merciless ridicule of Reginald Farrer.

The Garden's editorial carping at Kew put a serious strain on several of Robinson's friendships. That great gardener, the mild and scholarly Canon Ellacombe, wrote to Sir Joseph about what he called the damaging abuse of *The Garden*:

> "As to Robinson, I give up trying to set his twist right—but I regret it because I think his paper does good, though I care very little for it myself. Like Elwes and Maw I constantly threaten that I will send him no more notes, but he will not let us alone."

H. J. Elwes, gardener, forester, and traveller, and author, with Augustine Henry, of *The Trees of Great Britain and*

F

Ireland; and George Maw, before Mr. Bowles, the greatest authority on the genus crocus, were both among Robinson's most valuable contributors. And though he continued to carp he managed to keep them. Hooker himself seems to have taken no notice.

With Sir Reginald Blomfield the architect, on the other hand, his warfare was by no means one-sided. On paper Blomfield gave as good as he got—but the tide of taste ran with Robinson. Blomfield believed that a garden was no more and no less than an architectural adjunct or setting to a house. It should be a strictly formal affair of terraces and topiary. And, barring the actual digging in of such plants as might be needed—mere bricklayer's work—it was to be designed down to its last detail by an architect.

This arrogant claim enraged Robinson, who immediately published a reply in pamphlet form which was also incorporated in all later editions of *The English Flower Garden* and also, in case it should be missed, in his next book, *The Garden Beautiful*. He wielded a decidedly blunt instrument, but he wielded it with gusto; and by belabouring the whole surface of the target, he naturally from time to time hit the nail on the head. He was not concerned to defend, he attacked:

> "But the ugly buildings that strew the land everywhere—Georgian, carpenter's Gothic, Victorian—if we take away the good planting, the one saving grace about them, there will be nothing left but an ugly pile to laugh at. It is odd to see anyone writing on the subject without seeing that it is so."

In an elegant but ineffective reply, Blomfield complained with some justice that "Mr. Robinson is often florid, never precise".

In 1899 Robinson gave up the editorship of *The Garden*, passing it over to Gertrude Jekyll, who was mainly responsible for it for the next two years or so. Four years later he embarked on the most ambitious of his periodicals, *Flora and Sylva*. Writing on 1 December, 1903, he says:

> "Witness of the hot chase after process illustrations, small type, tin-shine paper, smudge lithographs, tomb-stone weights, and the less delightful features of modern books, the spirit of old things began to move in me and led at last to my going to the printer, who did not at first see my meaning. So I went home for Baskerville's Virgil, and asked him to get as near to it as he could in type, went with flower drawings to the best colour-printer in Europe; to the paper mills that still make real paper, and found surviving a wood-engraver who understood my good artist's drawings, and so began."

Robinson in his old age became fanatical about books. If they were not well produced by his expensive standards —which were never quite the same as Baskerville's— he would fling them unread behind the great back-log of his hall fire. The physical appearance of *Flora and Sylva* was ostentatious and uncertain. The type, in spite of Robinson's instructions, is not Baskerville, and he could not make up his mind whether or not what appears to be an 18-point Caslon looked well in double columns on his quarto page. The engravings are, in fact, reproduced by process blocks, and the coloured plates by H. G. Moon will not stand comparison with the best work of Sowerby or Curtis, nor even with Jane Loudon's. This was not the fault of the "best colour-printer in Europe", for there are a few pictures by other artists which have none of Moon's chocolate-box effects.

There is an element of vacillation also in the contents. Most of each monthly number was written by Robinson himself, and he had not, by this time, a great deal new to say. In fact, the magazine filled no obvious need, apart from a need felt by Robinson, and after three years he discontinued it. In the issue for December 1905 he wrote, with the hint of querulousness that was becoming characteristic:

> "*Flora and Sylva* has hitherto been published at less than its actual cost, with a view to putting little pecuniary bar to its circulation. It is now clear that a serial of the kind, done in the best way as regards illustrations, paper, and printing, does not appeal to a sufficient number of readers."

He had the unsold copies bound up in half-vellum and gave them as presents to his friends—and these bound volumes today fetch up to £30 a set.

In 1910, when Robinson was seventy-two years old, he became partially paralysed, losing the use of both his legs. This affliction had also befallen the old age of Thomas Rivers, the breeder of many new apples and new roses. For a man of Robinson's physical activity a future of bath-chair locomotion was extremely unattractive. He disliked machinery, but as soon as motorcars became at all common he got one; and immediately after the First World War he had specially made for him a sort of miniature motor-tractor with caterpillar wheels, in which he could drive himself, and sometimes a guest, over impossible ground into the remote recesses of his estate.

From year to year he continued to issue, through his

publisher John Murray, books, many of them little more than pamphlets, in the production of which Murray's experience acted as a brake on Robinson's more florid taste. Though, for that matter, in 1920 came a sort of companion to the earlier volume on Gravetye Manor. This was called *Home Landscapes*, and consists of thirty-two magnificent photographs of the landscape effects he had created round his Sussex home. Its production is certainly on the grand scale; as also is the sweeping style of its denunciation. Rival gardeners such as Sir George Sitwell and Mr. Samuel Parsons are dismissed with a contemptuous wave of the hand or with an impatient lecture —are compared, perhaps, to one who would recommend "a hundred ways to cook an egg or a herring, whereas there are only two or three good ways of cooking anything". But Murray's restraint showed itself in, for instance, *The Virgin's Bower*, a small book on the climbing varieties of clematis as grown at Gravetye, which is in every way a pleasing object to the eye. And about every alternate year there would be a new edition of *The English Flower Garden*. Robinson was famous. He was in *Who's Who*, where he describes himself briefly as "Author", with an incomplete list of his published works.

On 11 December, 1932, in spite of great age and great infirmity, William Robinson travelled thirty miles by road to attend the funeral of Gertrude Jekyll, who had died in her ninetieth year. Miss Jekyll was among his oldest and, in so far as he was ever intimate, his more intimate friends. He entertained at Gravetye, but he did not encourage intimacy. Perhaps he preferred plants to people.

Of his earlier friends, the most generally interesting, or at least the most widely known, was Ruskin. He probably knew Ruskin fairly well at one time. He certainly admired him inordinately. Unfortunately, though from the 'sixties onwards Robinson continually quotes Ruskin's books, he records only one brief fragment of his conversation: Ruskin and Robinson were discussing fruit trees in England as compared with those in warmer parts of the world, and Robinson remarked that in northern climates the fruit was always more beautiful than the flower; to which Ruskin replied, "Give me the flower and spare me the stomach-ache!" It also seems likely that Robinson was acquainted with William Morris, since Morris was sympathetic with the main Robinsonian principles and was personally known to Miss Jekyll.

Apart from Miss Jekyll, the friends with whom Robinson was on the easiest and most unreserved terms were Sir Frederick and Lady Moore, the son and daughter-in-law of Dr. David Moore of Glasnevin, the befriender of his youth. He sought their help in many things. It was on Sir Frederick Moore's advice that he decided to buy Gravetye Manor; and Sir Frederick, who had succeeded his father as Director of the Royal Botanic Gardens at Glasnevin, was one of the very few people to whom Robinson was prepared to defer on gardening matters.

Other friends were Mr. E. A. Bowles and Miss Ellen Willmott. Writing to Lady Moore in May 1931, he says: "I had no idea of seeing the Chelsea Show, but Miss Willmott has begged of me to go and I am going to-morrow." He was, by a few months, to outlive Miss Willmott also.

During his last years his active interest in his garden remained with him. "I pity that man," wrote Pope, "who has completed everything in his garden." Robinson would never have occasioned Pope's pity. At the age of ninety-five he was replanning an old orchard and planting a new one. He can hardly have enjoyed the fruits of these last labours, but that was not the point. And he lived on for nearly another two years in full possession of his faculties—motoring up to London early in 1935 to see an exhibition of pictures. On 12 May of that year he died peacefully, his last words being, "Children are always very delightful".

William Robinson was an original but more than commonly contradictory character. He was a firm vegetarian, though he did not impose his vegetarianism on his guests. As sometimes happens with vegetarians, he was also strongly set against the use of salt, mustard, and pepper; and he would always remove these from his table in any restaurant. One of his friends told me the strange story of a luncheon in Soho. Mr. Robinson had, as usual, placed the pepper and salt on a neighbouring table. During a long delay between one course and the next, he buttered himself a piece of bread. He then looked round irritably, rose in silence, picked up the pepper-pot from the table where he had put it, sprinkled pepper liberally on his bread-and-butter, returned to his own table, and, still in solemn silence, ate the lot. Nor was any explanation offered for this self-indulgent breach of an ascetic rule.

This sort of inconsistency was, to a great extent, characteristic. He lived a long life denouncing the formal garden; and his visitors were not unnaturally surprised to find that all the time he possessed a formal garden himself. He expressed a contempt for ostentation, yet occasionally he could be ostentatious to the verge of vulgarity. Unlike Miss Jekyll and many other gardeners, he had a genuine fondness for children, allowing them to play in his grounds, though he had contested their rights of way. Having no children of his own, Gravetye was left in his will to a somewhat neglectful Nation.

Perhaps he enjoyed surprising people. Before he

became, as Loudon said, "afflicted in the lower extremities", he used, whilst showing visitors his garden, suddenly to bend down and peer between his legs, saying that this was by far the best way of looking at a landscape or a plant, and urging his guests to try it. Skirts were worn long in those days, and there was apt to be a moment's awkwardness among the female sightseers. Perhaps his amusing inconsistencies and eccentricities were merely an expression of Irish fun. If so, it was his only continuing Irish characteristic; for in conversation all hint, tint, or tinge of a brogue or of Irish idiom had been got rid of and forgotten. His voice was the voice of a cultured Englishman, very soft until he grew excited or a little angry, which he easily did, when it would rise rather sharply and he would gesticulate with his long and well-shaped hands—creating thereby some suggestion of a French background.

As for Ireland, he never forgot the country, though he concealed the fact that he was born there. References to Ireland crop up continuously throughout his books. He compares the green Swiss meadows with the green Irish meadows. He recalls blue anemones in Irish woods. In later life he visited Ireland several times, travelling through the country; noting that natural gardens were still to be found there, but observing also that the land was "as bare of orchards as the back of a stranded whale" —a good Irish simile. In September 1932 he wrote, "I am sorry to see that hating one another for the love of God is still alive in Ireland."

Temperamentally, except in gardening, he was a conservative. He mistrusted innovations, particularly scientific innovations. His opinion of Darwin was uncompromising: "Evolution," he said contemptuously, "which explains how everything comes from nothing and goes back again to worse than nothing." And he referred to the evolutionists "who tell us how the Dandelion sprang from the Primrose some millions of years ago". In *Flora and Sylva* some Darwinian reference induced in him a quite ungrammatical splutter; but there also he published two well-informed articles in criticism of Darwin's work on the Cross-fertilisation of Plants. He was a connoisseur and a collector also of the more traditional kinds of painting—landscape and flower pieces, especially those of Fantin-Latour—"but we live in a time of much printed fog about artistic things". He was widely read in English literature, as one can tell from his quotations, and well read in French. In a letter to Lady Moore, written in 1933, he refers to his reading:

> "There has been much noise about George Moore, who came from Galway, and who tried his hand at the less delicate kinds of novels, but in his later years turned towards the way of the good English novelists. There are few novelists who read well, but one who is now dead, is Henry Kingsley. His books are mainly about Australia, but human and good. I knew him and liked him. He was a brother of Charles Kingsley. Many books come my way, but not many are readable. I hear a very good account of a lady writer who can speak Chinese well, and actually won their confidence to such an extent that she took up her living with a family in China. I should like to read her book. I hope I may find George Moore more readable than most Irish writers."

It is a lively letter for a man of ninety-five.

In his own writing, his early style is careful and self-conscious. It is in his later prose, flat and cumbrous as it often is, that one feels one sees Robinson as he was—downright, impatient, sometimes peevish. In his latest books his syntax is often slipshod, and his long wandering sentences are sleep-inducing. But, setting aside his own opinion, he does not require a reputation as a writer. As a person, when all is said and done, he was an Irish peasant boy who somehow became that impossible thing to become, an English Country Gentleman.

CHAPTER IV

THE ROBINSONIAN REVOLUTION

To those who knew William Robinson he seemed, as a person, an amiable or sometimes a not-so-amiable eccentric. As a gardener there can hardly be two opinions about his magnitude and importance. The English flower garden, as those now living have known it, is very largely what he made it.

In Loudon's time the old Landscape Gardening, the "naturalism" originally sponsored by Pope and Addison in a modest way, and extended vastly by their followers, was coming to an end. For one thing, with the rise of industrialism, you might find that your distant vista, appropriated only to your eye, had been sold by your neighbour and was being built over. Partly for such reasons, partly from a normal change of taste, gardening interest was beginning to focus round a new artificiality and a new formalism—the artificiality of the glasshouse, the formalism of the parterre of clipped hedges and carpet-bedding.

When Robinson came to England in the early 'sixties, carpet-bedding and bedding-out in general had gained everywhere a stranglehold. In his *Dictionary of Gardening*, published in 1885, George Nicholson describes bedding-out as "The temporary placing out of doors of green-house and other tender plants, during the summer months. It is considered by some to be the showiest, most expensive, and most unnatural style." As for carpet-bedding, Robinson himself defines it as

"a modification of bedding out, in which even the little bit of freedom that the plants show is suppressed. By pinching even the leaves, and by the selection of such plants as Stonecrops, House-leeks, and Echeverias, the bed is kept down to the carpet level. In the London parks one may often see men on planks, snipping off the little plants, and engaged on what seems to us work more of the tailor than the gardener."

It was this unnatural style that Robinson contended against—this, and topiary, and glasshouses. And he strove, successfully in the long run, to put in their place the herbaceous border and the wild garden.

It was by great good fortune that Dr. David Moore sent him to the Royal Botanic Society's garden and not elsewhere. For had he gone, let us say, to the Royal Horticultural Society's garden at Kensington he would have got there just in time to help lay it out in terraced beds of elaborate pattern. Or suppose he had gone to the Crystal Palace as a gardener, he would have found it in all its glory, "the most wonderful instance of modern gardening—water-temples, water-paths, vast stone basins". He might have been swept off his unsophisticated feet by so much magnificence, so much French theatricality, and never have seen that it was alien

to the English genius. As it was, he observed the
bedding-out:

> "The flower garden planting made up of a few kinds
> of flowers which people were proud to put out in
> thousands and tens of thousands, in patterns more or
> less elaborate in every garden save the very poorest
> cottage garden."

He saw the flower gardener "meanly trying to rival
the tile or wallpaper men". But he observed it all from
one of the few places where something else was being
done. Yet, though he admitted that the debt of
gardening to botany was great, and though more
than great was his own debt to the Botanic Society's
garden, he held that "the subordination of the garden
to Botany has been fruitful of the greatest evil to artistic
gardening". And of course it was not the Botanic
Society's garden as such that was important. What was
important was the opportunity his employment gave him
of seeing the unspoilt English cottage garden in the
unspoilt English country lane.

For here, in the humble plots of what was still a
peasantry, the tradition of natural planting, unaffected
by fashion or formality, had continued without a break
for untold generations. Robinson, in his search for native
plants with which to replenish the Botanic Society's wild
garden, saw cottage gardens such as those affectionately
described by Thomas Hardy in Dorset—where, the front
doors of the houses being mostly left open in the warm
autumn time,

> "through the long, straight entrance passages thus
> unclosed could be seen, as through tunnels, the mossy

gardens at the back, glowing with nasturtiums, fuchsias, scarlet geraniums, 'bloody warriors', snap-dragons, and dahlias, this floral blaze being backed by crusted grey stonework";

or such as that of Crabbe's East Anglian villager:

> Where grow the humble chives, and, hard by them,
> The leek with crown globose and reedy stem;
> High climb his pulse in many an even row,
> Deep strike the ponderous roots in soil below;
> And herbs of potent smell and pungent taste,
> Give a warm relish to the night's repast.
> Apples and cherries grafted by his hand,
> And clustered nuts for neighbouring market stand.
> Nor thus concludes his labour; near the cot,
> The reed-fence rises round some favourite spot;
> Where rich carnations, pinks with purple eyes,
> Proud hyacinths, the least some florist's prize,
> Tulips tall-stemmed and pounced auriculas rise.

They were the gardens of Miss Mitford's Berkshire, or such as were painted by Beatrix Potter and by Kate Greenaway. There was nothing like them in any other country. Certainly there was nothing like them in Ireland. They were Robinson's inspiration, or a large part of it, and years later, in 1892, he repaid something of the debt he owed them by founding and editing a half-penny paper, eight pages a week, called *Cottage Gardening*.

But the revolutionary ideas following from Robinson's first employment in England did not form themselves all at once in his mind. On his earliest visit to Paris for *The Times*, he looked with favour on the Jardin des Plantes and spoke with enthusiasm of it and of much else that he later came to reprobate. It is true he was never in two minds about Versailles. Between a Robinson and a Le Notre there was no possible point of accommodation.

To Loudon, Versailles had seemed "dreary beyond what could be imagined"; to Robinson it was appalling. Here was no small matter of conservatories and bedding-plants and clipped yew. On the contrary, here on a vast scale was something he had caught the merest reflection of in Paxton's Crystal Palace—"the theatrical gardening of Versailles reproduced in Surrey".

As he stood looking out from the garden façade, the prospect seemed to him "like that afforded by a suburban canal in a highly practical and unlovely country". In his reading he had noted "many dissertations on the several styles of laying out gardens", but here and now at Versailles, looking at one glance from words to things, as he says, it came into his mind

> "that there are really but two styles: one straitlaced, mechanical, fond of walls or bricks, or it may be gravel; fond also of such geometry as the designer of wall-papers excels in, often indeed of a much poorer and less graceful kind than that; fond too of squirting water in an immoderate degree, with trees in tubs as an accompaniment, and perhaps griffins and endless plaster and stone work. The other, with true humility and right desire though often awkwardly and blunderingly, accepting nature as a guide, and endeavouring to multiply, so far as convenience and poor man-power will permit, her most charming features."

The idea, conceived among the English villages, clarified on the façade at Versailles, was confirmed in the Swiss and Italian Alps. There, "above the cultivated land, flowers begin to occur on the fringes of the stately woods; they are seen in multitudes in the vast and delightful pastures with which many great mountain chains are robed, enamelling their soft verdure with innumerable dyes; and where neither grass nor loose herbage can exist; where feeble world-heat is quenched by mightier powers; where mountains are crumbled into ghastly slopes of shattered rock by the contending forces of heat and cold; even there, amidst the glaciers, they brilliantly spring from Nature's ruined battle-ground, as if the mother of earth-life had sent up her sweetest and loveliest children to plead with the spirits of destruction."

Which is in itself a flower of fine Ruskinian rhetoric. He fairly fell for these flowers of the European mountain ranges, and a little later for those, less beautiful, of the American Rockies.

In his book, *Alpine Flowers for English Gardens*, published in 1870, he continues to preach his new faith with fervour:

"With reference to the merits of alpine and allied types of gardening," he writes, "as compared with those commonly in vogue, there can be little doubt in the minds of all who give the subject any thought. On the one hand, we have sweet communion with Nature; on the other, the process which is commonly called 'bedding-out' presents to us simply the best possible appliance for depriving vegetation of every grace of form, beauty of colour, and vital interest. Visit any of our large country gardens, and probably the first thing that will be triumphantly told you is the number of scores of thousands of plants 'bedded out' every year, though no system ever devised has had a more miserable effect on our gardens."

This little blue-and-gold volume of Robinson's was, I think, the first book to lay down the right principles of Rock Gardening as they have been accepted by almost every writer on the subject since. Perfect drainage is insisted on. Unnatural rock-work is held up to scorn. "At Chatsworth, for instance, and also to some extent at the Crystal Palace, it might be supposed that rock-work and rock plants were never intended for each other's company." On the question of arranging the rocks themselves, he set, if possible, a higher standard than the fanatical Farrer:

> "The writer has seen a large rock-garden in the north of England which was laid with great care and at vast expense, and which is spoilt by one apparently small but fatal oversight—the dip of the beautifully arranged rockery-blocks is westerly and strongly marked, while the dip of the real 'live' rock immediately beneath is due east."

As to the ideal site for a rock-garden, Farrer and all later authorities have been content to repeat his recommendations almost word for word—without saying that they were his:

> "The position selected for the rock-garden should never be near walls; never very near a house; never, if possible, within view of formal surroundings of any kind. It should generally be in an open situation; and of course a diversified spot should be selected, if available. No tree should occur in or very near the rock-garden."

Some of poor Jane Loudon's rock-gardening suggestions are held up as object-lessons of what to avoid;
though, if it comes to that, she was more sensible than
most of her contemporaries.

Benjamin Maund, who had died but a few years
before Robinson's book appeared, is the classic example of
the pre-Robinsonian rock-gardener:

> "A level surface may be conveniently raised into
> inequalities; and deformities may be concealed; a
> variety of colour may also be obtained by the use of
> different materials, as gypsum, tufa, quartz, flints,
> fragments of limestone, granite, marble, or other
> hard rocks; also over-burnt bricks and refuse from
> iron-works may form prominent auxiliaries; in fact
> no material in stone is too rude for such use. If a rocky
> mound or raised border be required, the earth being
> first thrown together in the shape desired, it is but
> necessary to cover it in the rudest manner with such
> of the above-mentioned materials as can be obtained,
> and the picturesque may be made to reign where dull
> monotony previously existed. Those who cultivate
> small gardens may surprise themselves by their own
> creations out of such chaotic materials."

In such a *lapidarium*, direct descendant of the eighteenth-
century grotto, Maund proposed to grow *Sedum spurium*—
and it would be hard to find a place where *Sedum spurium*
will not grow.

That kind of rockery is what Robinson was out
against; and the extraordinary thing is, that that is what
Farrer and even later writers have been out against. For,
more extraordinary still, the Maund type of mound is
still being raised in suburban areas and in the grounds of
religious orders. There one may still see ferns and *sedums*

growing among lumps of melted glass, inverted tree-stumps, and occasional horse's skulls and shells. But Robinson at any rate ensured a more natural aim in all those gardeners—and rapidly their numbers grew—who took a serious interest in cultivating Alpine plants.

In the same year, 1870, Robinson followed up his blue-and-gold book on Alpine Flowers with a companion volume in green and gold called *The Wild Garden*.

The eighteenth-century garden had, as often as not, its intimate, romantical corner called the Wilderness, containing if possible a cascade or at least a spring, and a rustic cave or root-house such as might, with a little imagination, be the home of a hermit. The Wild Garden as Robinson conceived it, was no child, legitimate or illegitimate, of the picturesque Wilderness. The Wilderness had been nothing but an amusing, sophisticated episode in large-scale "landscape" work. The Wild Garden was to be a true garden of flowers. Robinson believed that the Mixed Border, by itself, could not quickly overtake and supplant the thirty-year-old bedding craze. There had been mixed borders, of a rather formal sort, it is true, in Loudon's day. What was wanted was something new which, by its very newness if not by its intrinsic merits, might in its turn become a popular craze. Rock-gardening, good in itself, was too specialized. But in his travels among the mountain regions of the Old World and the New he had seen many beautiful plants on the temperate lower slopes:

"not the wood and brake flora of any one alp or chain of alps, but that which finds its home in the immeasurable woodlands that fall in furrowed folds from beneath the hoary heads of all the great mountain chains of the world, whether they rise from hot Indian plains or green European pastures.

"The Palm and sacred Fig," he goes on, "as well as the Wheat and the Vine, are separated from the stemless plants that cushion under the snow for half the year, by a zone of hardier and not less beautiful life, varied as the breezes that whisper on the mountain sides, and as the little rills that seam them."

Robinson took pains to present his proposals in accents of engaging sentiment. And his proposals caught on. His idea was that these hardy exotics from temperate climates were, many of them, more suited for naturalisation in unmown grass along lake-sides at shrubbery edges, or in woodland glades, than for cultivation in even the most informal of herbaceous borders. Any garden of more than half an acre in size and more than half a century in age can still bear witness to the enthusiasm of Robinson's contemporaries for the new Wild gardening. The immediate difficulty, as he foresaw, was to lay hands on these hardy temperate exotics that he was praising. Up to that time the great plant collectors—men like Thomas Coulter, Robert Fortune, and William Lobb— had been sending home almost nothing but tropical plants for the various grades of greenhouse. It was only after Robinson had created a demand that a new generation of plant-hunters—Forest, Sargent, Augustine Henry, and later men like Wilson, Purdom, and Farrer—turned their attention to the "furrowed folds beneath the hoary heads of all the great mountains of the world", and there risked, and in some cases lost, their lives.

Meantime, Robinson was ready with a stop-gap suggestion. The first edition of *The Wild Garden* contains a long eighty-page essay on "The Garden of British Wild Flowers". He was exceptionally well equipped by his experience with the Royal Botanic Society to write on exactly this subject, and the essay is an able and persuasive account of all our surprisingly large number of garden-worthy native plants. By the time the second edition of the book was needed, eleven years later, the steady flow of suitable plants from Asia and America had set in, and Robinson most regrettably dropped this very charming chapter.

With these two books, the campaign was fairly launched. He was a solitary champion. His opponents were well dug in, and he did not have things all his own way. The nurserymen had by then what we now call a vested interest in the bedding-out system. So had the whole tribe of professional gardeners. But there were certain extrinsic factors working strongly for Robinson. Chief of these was the great expense, undiminished year in, year out, which the repeated raising and almost perpetual handling of bedding plants in the fashionable quantities involved. There was also the natural fickleness of fashion itself, and a veering of the *zeitgeist*. These and Robinson's ceaseless propaganda in his own books and gardening journals all helped to popularise the new gardening.

But the other side also was vocal. Among those who had in a sense a vested interest, if a less-mercenary one, with the opposition were certain Architects—notably John Dando Sedding and Reginald Blomfield. Sedding wrote a book called *Garden Craft*, and Blomfield one called *The Formal Garden*. Robinson rightly saw in these books an attack on all the ground he had regained from the formalists in twenty years of toil. He counter-attacked in a pamphlet on *Garden Design and Architects' Gardens*, published in 1892. Sedding had died before his own book appeared, but Blomfield was very much alive. His book was arrogantly high-handed. "The horticulturist and the gardener should work under control," he said, "and they stand in the same relation to the designer as the artist's colour man does to the painter, or as the builder and his workmen stand to the architect." Nothing could have been better calculated to enrage Robinson, and his pamphlet was furious and heavy-handed. There were plenty of chinks in Blomfield's armour, but Robinson did not bother about them, he simply laid on wherever he could get in a blow.

Blomfield replied in an elegant new preface to the second edition of his book. It was all very largely unnecessary. There was no need for Blomfield to have attacked Robinson's whole position, which in any case he did not understand. And Robinson, if he could have controlled his temper, might have shown Blomfield that there was potentially much common ground for them to cultivate:

"If there is any truth in his cant about nature would the landscape gardener bed out asters and geraniums, would he make the lawn hideous with patches of brilliant red varied by streaks of purple blue, and add his finishing touch in the magenta of his choicest dahlia? Would he plant them in patterns of stars and lozenges and tadpoles? Would he border them with paths of asphalt? Would he not rather fill his borders with every kind of beautiful flower that he might delight in and set them off with grass of pleasant green?"

That is Blomfield making passes with his rapier at Robinson. But Robinson never can have read so far, for here he hurls his bludgeon at Blomfield:

"It cannot be too clearly seen that 'Formal' gardens of the most deplorable type are things of our

own time, as it is only in our own time that the
common idea that there is only one way of making
a garden has been spread. Hence, in all the newer
houses we see the stereotyped garden often made in
spite of all the needs of the ground. Patterns of flowers
and carpet-beds are things of our own time; the most
formal and inartistic ways of arranging flowers that
ever came into the head of man."

He then goes on, fairly enough, to compare the bedding-
out that, unknown to one another, both he and Blomfield
hated, with the very similar "gravel gardens" of such
architects as Nesfield and Barry. On the whole, if one
can speak of winning, Robinson probably won. In any
case he was pleased with himself, reprinting his
pamphlet whenever a remotely appropriate occasion
occurred.

Wearing down the silent opposition of nurserymen
and the organisers of horticultural and flower shows was
a more tedious business, and to the end of his life Robinson
refused to compete or even to exhibit at shows, though he
used to go to them, and he sometimes consented to judge
at them. Gertrude Jekyll was of one mind with him about
their bad influence. Writing in *The Guardian* in 1896,
from which year she began to use her able pen in support
of his ideals, she said:

"Beauty, in all the best sense, is put aside in
favour of set rules and measurements, and the production of a thing that is of no use or value; and individuals
of a race of plants capable of producing the highest
and most delightful forms of beauty and of brightening
our homes, and even gardens, during the dim days of
early winter, are teased and tortured and fatted and
bloated into ugly and useless monstrosities."

And she complained that the sight of show flowers gave her a feeling of shame not unmixed with wrathful indignation.

This anti-exhibitionism was a logical consequence of the back-to-nature movement that Robinson was now leading. Another aspect of that movement was the campaign against clipped hedges and topiary work in general. And about this one cannot help feeling rather less sympathy; finding, surely, that topiary is on a different, a more respectable, footing than bedding-out —which was the original and main point of attack. For one thing, whereas bedding-out had begun only in the 'forties, topiary had a long tradition, a tradition of many centuries behind it. Further, anyone who had a mind to it could re-establish his bedding-out in a single season; but a finely clipped yew hedge, in perhaps elaborate and fantastic figures, though it could be destroyed in an hour, could not be renewed in a decade. But if the sculpture of living trees and shrubs was an art of ancient practice, so also the opposition to it was of some antiquity. Addison was against it. And Pope, writing, like Gertrude Jekyll, in *The Guardian*, but in 1712, published his witty and variously quoted "catalogue of Greens to be disposed of by an eminent Town-Gardener":

> "Adam and Eve in Yew; Adam a little shattered by the fall of the Tree of Knowledge in the great storm; Eve and the Serpent very flourishing.
>
> Noah's ark in Holly, the ribs a little damaged for want of water.
>
> The Tower of Babel, not yet finished.
>
> St. George in Box; his arm scarce long enough, but will be in a condition to stick the Dragon by next April.
>
> A green Dragon of the same, with a tail of Ground

Ivy for the present. N.B. These two not to be sold separately.

Edward the Black Prince in Cypress.

A Laurestine Bear in Blossom, with a Juniper Hunter in Berries.

A pair of Giants stunted, to be sold cheap.

A Queen Elizabeth in Myrtle, which was very forward, but miscarried by being too near a Savine.

An old Maid of Honour in Wormwood.

A topping Ben Jonson in Laurel.

Divers eminent modern Poets in Bays, somewhat blighted, to be disposed of a pennyworth.

A quick-set Hog shot up into a Porcupine, by being forgot a week in rainy weather.

A Lavender Pig, with sage growing in his belly.

A pair of Maidenheads in Fir, in great forwardness.

He also cutteth family pieces of men, women, and children, so that any gentleman may have his lady's effigies in Myrtle, or his own in Hornbeam."

Urbanity was no part of Robinson's make-up. He went bald-headed for the clippers of trees:

"What right have we to deform things so lovely in form? No cramming of Chinese feet into impossible shoes is half so foolish as the wilful and brutal distortion of the beautiful forms of trees.

"A gardener with shears in his hand is generally doing fool's work.

"Men who trim with shears or knife so fine a tree as the Holly are dead to beauty of form and cannot surely have seen how fine in form old Holly trees are. To give us such ugly forms in gardens is to show oneself callous to beauty and to prove that one cannot even see ugliness."

Yet, angry as he was, he had to admit that "occasionally we find clipped arches and bowers pretty, and these, when very old, are worth keeping".

There is no doubt that topiary work, which survived the pointed ridicule of Pope, has declined since Robinson wrote. Of course it is expensive to maintain "St. George in Box", clipping him with loving care three times a year; and even the delightful yew doves at Risley in Derbyshire —a county which, in its "gardens laid out by Paxton and his followers", Robinson reckoned among the most offensive in England—even these beautiful doves have probably long since gone, because of the cost of maintaining them. But also, Robinson's influence was, unaided by economics, very great. And it is likely enough that many a fine clipped hedge of holly or beech or yew was enthusiastically swept away—hedges that it has been found expedient, perhaps, now to replace with the quick-growing, insignificant, inferior *Lonicera nitida*. And one shudders to think how Robinson would have reviled that popular plant's short-lived shoddiness had he seen it in use.

If Robinson's distaste for exhibitions is at this date neither here nor there, since his own efforts have long since swept away the occasion of it; and if his topiary-phobia must be counted as spilt milk, useless to cry over; yet there remains in his reduction of the glasshouse a victory which one can wholeheartedly acclaim. For, at its best—at Chatsworth or at Alton Towers—there was little to be said for the horticultural-byzantine style of conservatory architecture. And anything less pretentious was merely mean. Glass of some sort is almost necessary in any garden, but it need not be a conspicuous feature;

and one hopes that never again will it occupy the entire field—as it did, so far as flowers were concerned, in the 1840s.

Robinson attacked the glasshouse ostensibly for two reasons: because it encouraged the growing of the wrong sorts of plants—it was of course an absolutely necessary adjunct to the bedders-out—and also because he found glasshouses, quite as much as clipped holly, an offence to the eye. As he says:

> "Apart from fine old houses and the landscape being defaced by the hard lines and colour of the glasshouse, there is the result on the flower garden itself; efforts to get plants into harmonious and beautiful relations are much increased if we have a horror in the way of glass sheds staring at us."

And once again he gets in a glancing blow at Paxton, pointing to "our Crystal Palace and Chatsworth, designed as they might be by a theatrical super who had inherited a millionaire's fortune".

All these engagements against hedge-clipping, flower shows, and glasshouses were incidents in the large-scale war against the bedders and carpet-bedders. Other contentions he had, such as a preference for wood fires and for urn burial, which were hardly connected with gardening. But his persistent propaganda against the use of Latin names, or at least in favour of the use of English names, for plants has some relevance though it was remote from the main issue.

This rather pig-headed preference for English names Robinson had taken over uncritically from Ruskin, with whom it was a matter less of bees in the bonnet than of bats in the belfry. Ruskin had explained in his *Proserpina* of 1875 that his purpose was "to interpret for young English readers the necessary European Latin or Greek names of flowers, and to make them vivid and vital to their understandings". He found that he could not do this in many cases because he thought "the most current and authoritative names are apt to be founded on some unclean or debasing association, so that to interpret them is to defile the reader's mind".

He therefore decided "to substitute boldly other generic names for the plants thus faultfully hitherto titled", and even "to mask those which there was real occasion to alter, by sometimes giving new names in cases where was no necessity of such kind". Some of the odd results of this morbid mentality were: Sedum acre turned into Stella domestica and given the English name of Roof-foil; Saxifraga changed to Francesca and translated to Rock-foil; Gentiana changed to Lucia and interpreted for young English readers as Lucy: "Lucy for Gentian because the king of Macedon, from whom the flower has been so long named, was by no means a person deserving of so consecrated a memory."

Goodness knows what Ruskin had in the back of his demented mind. There is one toadstool whose Latin name is an appropriate impropriety, but I can think of nothing else. A few gods and goddesses, nymphs and heroes, whose names may have been given to plants, were perhaps no better than they should be. But as for poor Gentius, his only recorded slip was to get himself defeated by Anicius Gallus in A.D. 169.

Robinson, who presumably had no Latin, probably took all this nonsense on trust. At any rate, he frequently shows concern for the weaker sex—"The multitude of Latin names means that women and children are barred by such nomenclature." And again, "Think of the British maiden or her mother struggling with such pedantic ugliness." And he had a veneration for *Prosperina* which he believed would be alive and well after all the little ephemera of the day had been forgotten.

Of course, apart from protecting the British maiden and her mother, there is a limited case to be made for the use of English names. It is partly sentimental, and none the worse for that. As Miss Mitford said, "One is never thoroughly sociable with flowers till they are naturalized, as it were christened, provided with decent, homely, well-wearing English names," but that is not to say that their Latin names are indecent, or that where a plant is not common enough to have an English name, one should invent an English name for it. To call snap-dragons *antirrhinums* is perhaps silly; but then, what shall one say of calling a Gentian a Lucy?

But besides sentiment, there is no doubt that the taxonomists, the systematic botanists, are a tiresome tribe. Is the genus of that plant with large leathery leaves saxifraga, or megassia, or bergenia? And the beginner, ordering *Iris unguicularis*, may be annoyed to find it the *Iris stylosa* that he always knew. And then there is, as Robinson complained, "the endless multiplication of varieties with cumbrous Latin names, of which we see an outrageous example in the Kew List". But except for the common traditional English names, there is every-thing to be gained by using the scientific binomials when referring to plants. And in the second part of *The English Flower Garden* Robinson does in fact index all his plants under their Latin names. It is one more fortunate example of his inconsistency.

There are two other causes in which Robinson was an advocate for innovations or reforms which were ultimately brought about. The first concerned "the dreadful mass of spiked iron railings" in the London parks and else-where. Writing in 1904, he suggested that

"even those who admire or who endure the sight of
iron railings would be almost alarmed if they knew
how many miles of them there are in Hyde Park—
a waste of metal. They destroy the good effect of the
Serpentine from many points of view. If the park is
only to be considered as a run for town-imprisoned
dogs, the railings must be kept, but quite half of the
iron might even then be done away with. Park or
garden beauty that can only be seen through spiked
railings is bought at too high a price."

Some forty years later, under the stress of total war, what
he wanted was done. And now, in 1950, such are the
depredations of London's hooligans, the iron railings
must be replaced.

The second matter on which, also in 1904, Robinson
spoke was the securing of large areas in the wilder
parts of the British Isles as National Parks or Nature
Reserves.

"The only difficulty," that Robinson saw,
"would be to prevent such parks from becoming mere
places of public resort, which would destroy all the
quiet for the creatures we would encourage in them.
This, he thought, might best be avoided by selecting
spots difficult of access and remote from busy centres.
The woods in such should also be closed at certain
seasons of nesting and breeding, and the mere sight-
seer excluded altogether from certain parts."

These words might almost have been taken from the
Report on the Conservation of Nature in England and
Wales presented to Parliament by the Minister for Town
and Country Planning in July 1947. Another great gain

that Robinson expected from these National Parks was
"that they might afford opportunity for planting our
native trees in bold natural masses and forests". In fact
he foresaw—what the National Trust has actually provided—renewed scope for the Landscape Gardener.
Unfortunately, there is at present no gardener with
Robinson's forceful character and broad grasp. The
architects have seen their chance, and the term that is
now in use is "landscape architect" instead of what
Robinson spoke of as "the good word 'landscape-gardener'
used by Loudon and Repton and many other excellent
men".

In his later years Robinson's interest in Landscape
Gardening grew. His last important horticultural book,
The Garden Beautiful, deals almost entirely with forest trees
and their large-scale planting. Among trees, as in most
things, he had his plain-spoken preferences. He detested
monkey-puzzles and welingtonias, and he loved the
larch, "The best tree that ever came to us from oversea,"
he called it at a time when it was far from popular. "All
men speak ill of thee, unlucky Tree," as F. W. Faber
wrote in one of his almost first-rate sonnets. And he too,
like Robinson, praised it:

> Thy boughs it is that teach the wind to mourn,
> Haunting deep inland spots and groves forlorn
> With the true murmurs of the plaintive sea.
> When tuft and shoot on vernal woodlands shine,
> Who hath a green unwinterlike as thine?
> And when thou leanest o'er some beetling brow,
> With pale thin twigs the eye can wander through,
> There is no other tree on earth but thou
> Which brings the sky so near or makes it seem so blue.

As among trees the larch, so among flowers the michaelmas daisies were his favourites. Starworts he called these

stiff and uninspiring Americans, and at Gravetye he formed an almost complete collection of all the garden varieties—man-made varieties at that.

And this was unlike him. For of Robinson's basic principles one can only say that they amounted to a philosophy, and that he was a thorough-going "naturalist". Just as he could not bear to see a tree trimmed by the shears, so he always disliked anything so unnatural as grafting, and the Gravetye roses were all grown on their own roots. All the same, he considered gardening an Art and himself an Artist. Here too he held vigorous opinions, with no nonsense about the artist expressing his "personality" or any such thing. Less rightly, perhaps, he thought that art had nothing to do with "invention". "True art," he said, "is based on clear-eyed study of and love for Nature," and, "The work of the artist is always marked by its fidelity to Nature." On this question, though his opponents made debating-points against him, he was more consistent than on most—praising the paintings of Fantin-Latour and the Barbizon school above all others.

In laying out a garden he would have no preconceptions—"Plans should be made on the ground to fit the place, and not the place made to suit some plan out of a book", which is only a sober statement of the poet Shenstone's ruling that the "Ground should first be considered with an eye to its peculiar character: whether it be the grand, the savage, the sprightly, the melancholy, the horrid, or the beautiful." Like the eighteenth-century gardeners also, he believed that there was a connexion between landscape painting and garden design, though for him the test of a good garden was, not that it should resemble a known picture, but that a good artist should wish to paint it. "Through all the rage of the 'bedding-out' fever, it was impossible for an artist to paint a garden like those which disfigured the land from Blair Atholl to the Crystal Palace."

Yet Robinson was neither a fool nor a fanatic. He admitted that formality in some places was necessary: "The flower garden itself near the house must be laid out with formal beds, or else we cannot cultivate the flowers or get about the grounds with ease." This was a step towards William Morris's liberal opinion, expressed in *Hopes and Fears for Art*, that "large or small, the garden should look both orderly and rich. It should be well fenced from the outer world. It should by no means imitate either the wilfulness or the wildness of Nature, but should look like a thing never seen except near a house." But there the operative word is "imitate": Morris, no less than Robinson, believed that a growing plant should grow naturally, and, mediaevalist though he was, he was in general sympathy with the gardening practice of the anti-formalists.

Robinson was an active force in gardening for nearly seventy years. He was a born fighter, and he contended, unrelenting, against Paxton and Paxton's persistent ghost, against George Glenny, an able gardener who would have fixed the forms of flowers according to something like a Platonic Idea, and against the Philistine host of bedders, clippers, and contorters. During much of this time, almost single-handed, he maintained the true genius of English gardening, and ultimately brought its practice back to the true tradition.

It is not, of course, that all the other gardeners were bedders-out. In particular there were certain gardening families who were quite untouched by the bedding craze. But the Moores were at Glasnevin in Ireland and so were ill-placed to influence events in England. The Ellacombes were country clergymen whose passion was in growing plants, and to whom garden design and floral colour-

H

schemes were not remotely interesting. Finally there were the Hookers at Kew; but the Hookers, though, unlike the Moores, they controlled a great central garden, were essentially academic botanists rather than gardeners.

So it is fair to say that if our gardens can still recognize their ancestry in such an eighteenth-century garden as Moses Browne's, who asked:

> What white can match my Lily's virgin snows?
> What red, the crimson of the blushing Rose?
> What regal purple with the Scabious vie?
> Or scarlet match the Poppy's flaming dye?
> What yellow, lovely as the golden morn,
> The Lupine and the Heliotrope adorn?
> How mix'd a hue the streaky Tulip stains!
> How curious the Carnation's marbled veins!
> Ethereal blue the silky Violets wear!
> And *all* unite their sweets in mingling air;

if we have escaped from the kind of garden you find in some of Miss Broughton's novels, where "the scentless flame of the geraniums and calceolarias fills, without satisfying, the eyes"; if, on the contrary, it is no uncommon thing to find gardens like Miss Sackville-West's:

> Seemingly wild, yet not too wild, too rough;
> An art in wildness, even in the bluff
> And thorny branches of the hedgerow May,
> Red, rose, or white; or in the cloudy puff
> Of ceanothus, blue and powdery;
> Or hedge of roses, growing devil-care,
> —Rose of the World; th' embroidered Tuscany;
> The scented Cabbage, and the Damascene;
> Sweet-briar, lovelier named the eglantine;

But above all the Musk
With classic names, Thisbe, Penelope,
Whose necterous load grows heavier with the dusk
And like a grape too sweetly muscadine;

If this is so, then it is fair to say that our escape from
aberrations and our return to tradition is mainly due to
the genius of William Robinson.

CHAPTER V

REGINALD FARRER AMID SNOW AND ICE

No consideration of the background of modern gardening, however brief, could avoid taking notice of Loudon and Robinson. They are egregious in the old sense. They stand out as the main agents by whom an ever-changing but never completely broken gardening tradition has been transmitted. But these great professional gardeners did not supply all the ingredients that have gone to make the gardening theory and practice of today. That theory and practice could never have developed as far and as fast as it has done without the enormous number of new plants introduced during the last 150 years.

Of the many plant-hunters and plant-collectors to whom we owe these introductions, I myself do not know to whom we are most indebted. If I choose Farrer to represent them, it is because he was an important collector and also an important gardener and, beyond these, a voluminous and attractive writer—at least, like it or not, no page that he wrote can be read without the reader's attention being attracted to his style.

Loudon was Scotch and Robinson was Irish, and both came from humble households. Unlike them then, Reginald Farrer was an Englishman. And unlike them also, he was the son of well-to-do parents on the fringes of the aristocracy. He was born in February 1880 at his family's old home under the great mountain of Ingleborough in Yorkshire. He was born with a hare lip, causing an impediment in his speech which he never more than partially overcame, and which during his childhood was sufficiently incapacitating to prevent his being sent to school. He was, however, rather more than averagely well educated at home.

Before he was ten he was a sharp-eyed field botanist and he also had a fair knowledge of plant anatomy. At fourteen he began making his first rock-garden in a disused quarry. This garden, afterwards referred to in his writings as "the old rock-garden", was not, by his high standards, a permanent success, though he always maintained it in cultivation. In the same year, 1894, he made his first published contribution to horticultural literature with a note in *The Journal of Botany* on *Arenaria gothica* which he had found growing on Ingleborough—its only known British habitat. This not very exciting little sandwort was ever afterwards dear to him—dear, too, to those who purchased it in later years from his Craven Nursery —and he always vigorously defended its status as a true British Alpine plant against all and sundry who supposed it a mere recent importation, perhaps with a cargo of timber, from Norway.

When he was seventeen, Farrer went up to Balliol College, Oxford. It is tempting to think that something of his Oxford life—his mental life and the moulding of his opinions, at any rate—is reflected, with inevitable

× 1897

distortion, in some of his novels. He was certainly an unconventional young man, though he can hardly have been such a freak as his Michael Hallibon in *The Ways of Rebellion*. In any case, he came down from the University in 1902 with a second in Mods, and a third in Greats; and next year he set off for Japan, where he was joined by two English friends.

Before returning to England by way of Canada, Farrer lived in Tokio, renting a house with Japanese servants for about eight months. And he wrote an account of his impressions and adventures in a most engaging book, *The Garden of Asia*, published by Methuen in 1904—not, indeed, that his adventures were of a hair-raising kind compared with what frequently occurred to him on his later travels. But he tells delightfully of his wanderings round the pavement booths at night, turning over the attractive rubbish they displayed—old odds and ends that were things of beauty to his curious and fastidious eye; and of the gardens that were everywhere mingled with the streets where he found in the curves of the Dwarf Trees a quality which he elsewhere found only in the impeccable curves of a paragraph by Jane Austen.

During his stay in Tokio Farrer had an entirely charming affair with a geisha girl—one of those learned and accomplished Japanese women whom it would be ridiculous to think of as prostitutes. And to the memory of his lovely and sympathetic Lady Little Willow Tree he was ever after faithful. For at twenty-three he is already word-wise and sagely disillusioned. "Nothing," he writes, "is less stable, no guide more delusive and treacherous than that which the young call love, and the old, more wisely, instinct." So he moralised, moustachioed and tending to fat; and in the shelter of that grave opinion he appears to have remained.

Farrer was ever restless, and his house in Tokio was a

base from which he explored not only the length of Japan but the Asiatic mainland of Korea, when he made a four- or five-day trip into China as far as Peking itself. This was his first footing of that vast country which was to be the scene of his greatest exploits as a plant-hunter and botanist.

None of Farrer's journeys were botanical to the eclipse of other interests. In this Oriental expedition the other interests—and they were many—preponderated above the yet-frequent recordings of plants and gardens. China and Japan laid hold on his imagination—China, as it proved, with the more permanent appeal. China in the early years of this century was still, totteringly, imperial; and, for all his Liberalism, antique custom, and long-drawn tradition meant much to Farrer. Outside Peking he came to a ruined palace of the Empress Dowager. There, meditating in its deserted gardens, he repeopled them with past inhabitants:

"The place is so dead and calm that its effect is one of cold artificiality. The winding paths are not really empty, the palace not indeed a desert. Along those shores in the heavy silence go bright people of long ago. The hush is so vivid that one can hear the rustle of those rich silks laid useless now in mildewed coffers. The wanderer is an intruder by that quiet shore. That calm lake—those gardens with their pines and rockeries; those summer pavilions that stand slowly lapsing into the unruffled water, those beds of lotus, those pale reflections of the hills—belong not to him, but to others long vanished, whose voices still throng the stillness. About the winding ways go precious dead women upon whom we have no right to look—queens, empresses, and mothers of queens, passing delicately by on silken feet; great ladies, fan

in hand for the pleasure of their princesses; high
nobles and lords-in-waiting privileged into the holy
garden of their sovereign; and in their sacred glories
the pale phantoms of emperors that are not, to us
that behold, so much as a name upon a grave. The
wanderer passes silent from the lake of unearthly
silences—the lake immemorially sad with the tranquil
sorrow of a thing whose fate has long been written,
signed, and sealed."

Such prose, with its echoes of Pater and the nearer
'nineties, seems to have come naturally to him whenever
he was deeply moved. Some of the set passages in his later
books are even more self-consciously and more purpuri-
ally orchestrated, but his characteristic style, in all its
flexibility, was his from the start. He could do with it as
he pleased, adapt it to any occasion. He disliked Japanese
food, and it may be that his vegetarianism dates from the
discovery that his pet kitten had, on the previous day,
appeared before him as *fricassee* of chicken. But even
Japanese food had its surprises. There was a little bun
bought for one farthing:

"From far away across the abysses of time comes
back the haunting memory of that brown bun. She
is light and misty in composition, and her flavour is
of toffee, strangely subtilised. She is, as Webster
declares our mortal life to be, 'mere crudded milk
fantastical puff paste', crumbling and evanescent as
the beauties of youth. To eat her is to eat some
delicious dream; she is flaky with the sweet crispness
of a clear vision, and, passing, she leaves a tender
recollection of a dear treasure loved and lost."

On Queens long dead, or on brown farthing buns
(with what real references to Lady Little Willow Tree),

Farrer's prose was a medium through which he could express his feelings with perfect modulation. It is only when he has no feelings but must needs write, when, in fact, he is bored, that he becomes careless and unexpectedly slipshod, prolix, and tautological. Nor, luckily, was his buoyant spirit often bored.

Having returned to England with the manuscript of *The Garden of Asia* in his Gladstone bag, Farrer settled down, not immediately to the cultivation of his garden, but with the ambition to become a novelist, a poet, and a dramatist. *The Sundered Streams* appeared in 1905, *The House of Shadows* in 1906, *The Ways of Rebellion* in 1908, and *The Anne-Queen's Chronicle*, and *Through the Ivory Gate* before 1911. He also published during these years his two poetic plays, *The Dowager of Jerusalem* and *Vasanta the Beautiful*.

Of Farrer's novels and, even more certainly, of his poems, one must admit that not by them could oblivion have been kept at bay or by many days delayed. He wrote them when he was young and when he lacked the self-discipline and self-abnegation that, as he well knew, is demanded by their Muses. His fiction reads as wish-fulfilling day-dreams, an adolescent, inexperienced mixture of cleverness and silliness with characters that are more-than-life-size marionettes jerking and creaking through sometimes amusing but nearly always ill-connected episodes.

One of his typical heroines was endowed with the

"beauty which is never young and never old—a crystal glory of loveliness, calm and cool and pale, with exquisite clear-cut features, smiling eyes, and hair of a crisp pure gold. She carried herself with a singular erectness, and her face was poised at a delicate ironic slant upon the long back-drawn throat."

And this paragon of loveliness was, not unreasonably, maddened by the prig of a hero who declined all her advances. "Ha, Michael!" cried Eleanor, with a snarl, "you harangue me like a preacher." And so they go, these novels, satire alternating with melodrama, to their unlikely ends. The best of them is *The Anne-Queen's Chronicle*, for there the fact that the heroine is the historical Anne Boleyn imposes a check on Farrer's wayward fancy.

Conspicuous failure as a novelist is not surprising, considering Farrer's temperament. What does surprise is his acute and critical appreciation of the novelist's art in others—particularly Jane Austen. She was his favourite author, and he never stirred abroad unaccompanied by a set of her novels. In 1917 he wrote a "Jane Austen Memorial Article" for the *Quarterly Review*. This essay is full of understanding, and of just appreciation—of Jane Austen in particular, and of what was required of the novel in general.

> "The essence of conviction in the game of make-believe," he says, "is to convince yourself entirely, by blotting out the whole irrelevant world from your purview, and centralising, with a single-eyed undeviating passion of conviction, upon the tale you are setting out to live."

And he considered that "the whole point of reading lies in eager co-operation with a sympathetic writer".

He praised Jane Austen for not tearing a passion to tatters—which was precisely his own besetting fault—and for being a clear-brained rather than a red-blooded writer. He liked her because she appreciated women so perfectly, and so inexorably revealed them. Between himself and Jane Austen he felt, in fact, an emotional affinity. All the same, his analysis of each of her novels is masterly in its unemotional intelligence.

He had, too, a proper appreciation of the Elizabethan dramatists; but this did not save him from the embarrassing puerilities of *The Dowager of Jerusalem*, a poetic play that reads like an ill-advised, because boring, burlesque of Webster or Turnour.

However, if Farrer was a novelist and poet *manqué*, it does not matter, since he himself realised his mistake in time, and realised, too, where his true, his unique, talents lay—in gardening, in writing about gardening, and in collecting new plants from the ends of the earth for gardens. Every year from the time he left Oxford, when he was not travelling in more distant lands, he visited one or other of the Alpine ranges of Europe. He was a man of restless vitality, physical and mental. He was by no means untiring but, given a sleep in comfort—and no one had a truer appreciation of comfort—or a few chapters of Jane Austen, he had a capacity for rapid recuperation.

In 1907 he published *My Rock Garden*, his most popular and influential book, and the only one of his works to be kept continuously in print for more than forty years.

In that year also he paid a visit to Ceylon. This was a good deal briefer than his visit to Japan, and the book he wrote about it, *In Old Ceylon*, has none of the intimacy that makes *The Garden of Asia* so attractive. The book begins with one of Farrer's literary *tours de force*, an account of the native precious stones and the jewel-shops of Colombo —brilliant, lustrous pages, describing, as few beside him could describe, objects that dispassionately delighted his eye. He had done much the same for prostitutes in Tokio, and he was to repeat the feat many times, and always freshly, for the flower-foamed meadows of the great mountains. But the style of the book's first few pages could not be maintained, and Farrer was too good an artist to attempt to maintain it. For the rest, *In Old Ceylon* is a discursion on Cinhalese religion, history, literature, and art. He deals in it hardly at all with his own adventures and activities, and the book is the only one of his non-fictional writings that has no interest for the gardener.

Besides *In Old Ceylon*, Farrer published in 1908 a novel, a drama, and, what was more to the point, a book called *Alpines and Bog Plants*—a sort of sequel or companion volume to *My Rock Garden*. The mere thought of the industry and energy put into the writing of so many pages and chapters makes one feel uncomfortable. It would take all a normal man's time. But Farrer was doing other things as well. Practical gardening and plant-collecting, to say nothing of a vast amount of miscellaneous reading—these, too, were done—done well and with exuberance.

His exuberance almost bubbles over when he is conducting an imaginary but sympathetic visitor on a kind of butterfly's-eye view of his own garden. Only towards the end of his book, *In a Yorkshire Garden*, is the lyric twitter muted. He leads his visitor or reader into "Alice's garden", saying that who or what Alice was it is no part of his contract to explain. But he points to the green mound where, plucked before her prime, she lies eternally, bloomed about by his choicest flowers; and the writing or conversation takes up a wistful, elegiac note. The book, apart from some valuable gardening information, is not among Farrer's best.

He was, in fact, rather over-writing. And he himself may have felt that he was. For, from 1909 to 1912 he did very little literary work, and plunged himself instead into party politics.

If Farrer was mistaken in thinking himself a novelist, he was more deeply, doubly, deluded in thinking himself a politician. Intellectually, it is true, he held liberal principles, but he held them with a tinge and tint of ironical emotion which was alien, and surely alienating, to the high seriousness, the superior moral aim, of the Liberal Parliamentary Party. He was too sceptical and too witty.

"Why does one *ever* want to see things, handle things, possess things?" he asks. "For all these matters are illusion and disappointment; the one real and fulfilling sight, touch and possession, is that which lies in thought only. For in thought lies the only possible realisation that can last and satisfy. There is a notable gospel to go and preach to the poor and the meek. How very much nicer for them, and more popular, to be told they shall inherit the earth, although everybody (themselves included, for that matter) knows perfectly well that they never will do any such thing; and that we all mean to take jolly good care they don't."

There is plenty of evidence that Farrer, with the whole mystical and religious side of him—and it was quite a large side—believed these sentiments; but they were unlikely to commend him to Liberal party organisers.

However, in the 1911 election, when for the last time Liberal parliamentary fortunes were at the flood—before they sank for ever—he contested the Ashford Division in the Liberal interest, and was satisfactorily defeated. He may have been disappointed. He ought not to have been surprised. It may have been some consolation to him that in the local government elections he was returned to the Yorkshire County Council. Thereafter he troubled himself no further in practical politics.

In the summer of the year before his political miscarriage, Farrer had gone for what he called "a cheap little humble trip of six weeks or so round the Graian, Cottian, and Maritime Alps", dreaming of the vast Asiatic mountain masses that he then, and how mistakenly, supposed he would never visit. The book in which he tells of this trip, *Among the Hills*, is one of his most delightful. For part of the time Mr. E. A. Bowles was his companion, and there were others at whose expense he occasionally makes merry—thereby also making enemies.

No one had a sharper sense of the ridiculous than Farrer, and no one was better than he at depicting and framing easily isolated episodes. He had a precise eye for the picturesque, which was the ruination—or one of the ruinations—of his novels, and the making of his travel books, especially when, in his travel books, the picturesque was a setting for the picaresque. On 10 July he set out from Cuneo to Valdieri in a victoria along a road "perfectly straight, and as flat as a Bishop's biography". He had been warned that the hotel he was bound for would not yet have opened for the season. "This of course, was nonsense, as the hotel always opens on the third of July."

With nightfall the fireflies appeared, and still the victoria crawled on through the darkness. Then the road which had begun with such episcopal flatness became a stone slope flanked with banks of snow. And so, ever more slowly, on, until "down at the blackest heart of the blackness I began to feel, half-doubting, something like a dim blur of a darkness less intense". A moment later the driver

"waved his whip and told me that these were the Baths of Valdieri. Through a deathly stillness we drove across a bridge and up to the front of the hotel. I could discern an arcaded frontage, and a mass of masonry like a mountain. One could only see a yard or so. What one divined from this was almost terrible in its immensity. And still no light, no sound anywhere, no sign of life. It was wonderful and ghastly to stand there in the midnight, outside that closed barrack in the heart of the mountains. It was so wonderful that one almost forgot one's anguish. . . . I dismounted, realizing that everybody must have gone to bed. I climbed broad flights of stone steps, into an open empty hall. It was a pillared colonnade like a Pharaoh's Palace, with arches carried indefinitely far above our heads, on columns vast as those of a Cathedral. We wandered up and down the dim expanse, shouting into the silence. The flame of the carriage lamp wavered among the blacknesses, and showed us to each other like pismires roving on the floor of cavernous night itself. And still nothing happened. On and on I wandered, down the arcade, to where I thought I saw a glimmer: nothing. At the back the arcade led to a staircase, where a gigantic clock ticked awfully. But still no sign of life. The driver wandered away at last, to try and find some living creature, perhaps in the caretaker's cottage. I was left alone in that weird catacomb, crushed by the sense of its black immensity. The Gesso river roared outside in the darkness, deep down in its bed, and the ticks of the giant clock reverberated with a hollow sound through the empty world. Otherwise I might have been sitting lone in the ruins of great Babylon. And that ticking only emphasised the solitude; the echoing of my footsteps on the stone-flags was disturbing and terrible."

From this fragment of a Gothic Romance, this nightmare out of *The Castle of Otranto* or *The Mysteries of*

Udolpho, he was rescued by the return of his driver with a sleepy porter. And for some days Farrer was a solitary and none-too-welcome guest in the unopened empty echoing hotel.

Farrer's object in visiting Valdieri at that time was to seek, successfully as it turned out, for *Saxifraga florulenta*, "the oldest and loneliest of Saxifrages", and a plant so inaccessibly rare that its continued existence had from time to time been doubted. His enthusiasm and delight in botanical discovery are the main theme of this book— a theme which ought not to weary even the unbotanical reader, so skilfully is it set off by accounts such as that of the arrival at Valdieri, or by fragments of curious learning; not the sort of learning you find in *Baedeker*, but the odds and ends with which he delighted to store his memory. So that when he came to the town of Tenda he naturally recalls that

> "there are but few places in Europe over which Mary Tudor was not one time Queen, Countess, or Duchess. Tenda is not among them; blended in the duchy of Milan, it should add yet another to the weight of crowns that brought so much glory and so small profit to that weary little red head. It is seldom indeed that the plant-collector in Europe can escape the ubiquitous royalty of Queen Mary."

The Tudors, especially Henry VIII, his wives and daughters, fascinated Farrer; and they, with Jane Austen, tend to crop up in the most unlikely places in his books.

In 1913 Farrer published *King Laurin's Garden*, which deals with another plant-hunting visit, this time to the Dolomites where again Mr. Bowles went with him—to be inoculated with Farrer's passion for primulas. And

Reginald Farrer

then, in that same year, he set out on the first of his great central Asian expeditions.

On this journey among the Tibetan Marches and the mountainous Chinese province of Kansu, he had as his only European companion William Purdom, a young man of magnificent physique, an experienced plant-hunter, an excellent photographer, and in every way the best possible associate, the "absolutely perfect friend and helper", for the rather exacting and incalculable Farrer. Purdom, after training at Kew, had, four years previously, collected for the firm of Veitch over part of the district to which he now returned as guide. He never came back to England. In 1915 he took service as a forestry expert under the Chinese Government, and died suddenly in China in 1921. His name is perpetuated in a number of new plant species.

The adventures and successes of the Purdom-Farrer expedition during its first year, from March to November 1914, are recorded by Farrer in what he spoke of as a "succinct and laconic work" in two portly volumes of over 600 pages entitled *On the Eaves of the World*. These were followed by another similar volume called *The Rainbow Bridge*, into which is compressed the billowing story of the second year's work.

These three volumes form, from the purely literary point of view, Farrer's most ambitious undertaking, as was the expedition they record by far his most important.

In its horticultural and botanical results these two years of arduous collecting were a triumph. At altitudes often well over 10,000 feet above sea level on those monumental mountains, and in the damp depths of their ravines, climbing among "enormous boulders like scattered churches", they gathered not only a rich harvest of new and horticulturally exciting plant species, but a

I

rich harvest also of entertaining and often perilous adventures.

Again and again the landscape called up Farrer's most magniloquent descriptive powers:

> "The cauldron of screes and shingle-slides and stone-tumbles that converge in a tumult of desolation from the cirque of the Thundercrown precipices is a wild and weird spot. Chaos and a huge gaunt splendour are the keynotes of the place. Far overhead all round, you are gloomed down on by naked peaks and ridges from which the sweeps of stone descend in grand stern lines, interspersed with rare strips of dark tussocky moorland turf, in which occasionally flames the violet of the imperial Primula."

Such was the common countryside—a countryside in which anything might happen and almost everything did, from gentians to bandits, and from Living Buddhas to broken bridges. Bridges, indeed, were the despair of the party. In drenching rain they came to one, spanning an ice-cold foaming torrent. Spotted Fat, Farrer's horse,

> "sniffed at the bridge for a moment, and then began solemnly to advance step by step, picking his way delicately from rickety pole to pole. Beneath me, far down between the gaps of the planks, I could see the boiling, ice-grey water. . . . Suddenly I became aware that Spotted Fat was sliding out towards the un-protected edge. . . . A paralysis possessed me as I felt his hind-quarters swinging out more and more perilously. Purdom's frozen face of horror advancing to meet me remains photographed on my mind as the last thing I remember ere, incredulous to the last, I was conscious of a stumbling subsidence behind me, a

splintering crash, and . . . Spotted Fat and I were falling, falling through twenty feet of emptiness, and down into the glacial abysses of the river. . . . Desperately I struck out at each rocky headland as it raced into sight, and raced away behind me again out of reach. They came and passed with the uncanny quick elusiveness of nightmares, seeming to be held out to be withdrawn again at once, like things slid in and out of the wings of a theatre. I could study the Primulas in their crannies as they fled blandly by. My latter end was already plainly in sight, but no high and holy thoughts possessed me. . . . Instead I was consumed only with rage over so ignominious a conclusion, a rage that even extended to Purdom, who meanwhile was hopping along from promontory to promontory with cheerful smiles and shouts of encouragement. The least he could have done, I felt, was to jump in and perish also. . . . Spluttering my indignation to the high gods, I was whirled straight towards the race, and abandoned hope; when suddenly I felt the point of a rock beneath my toe. Frantically I sought lodgement on it, but could not stand against the flood, and in an instant was torn onwards, only immediately after to come to rest . . . on a long wide shallow where not so much as a kitten could easily have drowned. Purdom, in fact, had all along seen this quite inevitable rescue, and the whole drama was dissipated."

Whether Farrer enjoyed his forced bathe or not, he certainly enjoyed writing an account of it, which is here reduced to about a quarter of its elaborately embroidered length.

And there were adventures of the mind, too. From time to time they visited and rested in some great Buddhist monastery, presided over by a learned Abbot and secluding from the world, perhaps, a Living Buddha.

From the time of his first visit to Japan, Farrer had been deeply interested by the Buddhist religion. I have been told by one who knew him slightly that he became a convert to Buddhism. He had certainly a strong bent towards religious speculation, but it is not clear that he ever had any notable religious experience. He had a contempt for most of the Christian missionaries he met with, and out of politeness, at the least, he took part in the religious services of the Buddhist monasteries.

But of the religious practices of the monks he said, "How much nonsense and how much sound primeval sense there may be in all these antics let someone else decide, and on the extent to which material acts, if sincere in intention and sufficiently intense of purpose, can react on the spiritual world." Farrer was genuinely religious in that he believed in spiritual realities, and in the supernatural power of holiness—such holiness as he found sometimes in these remote monasteries. But he had little patience with dogmatically exclusive theologies: "Either all prayers and formulae have equal possibilities of validity, or none have any at all," he said; and the holding of that liberal opinion must have precluded his adherence to any single sect.

Before the collectors' first year was over, war had broken out in Europe. On 4 August, 1914, Farrer and Purdom were sitting in their camp on the slopes of a Tibetan mountain, looking out on the passionless persistence of the rain. They were, naturally, un-informed of the more distant and more dismal events then occurring. And if they had been, they, no more than the rest of the world, could have known that Night was falling on the long Day—an era of 200 years—whose Classical Age was the eighteenth century, whose Hellenistic period was the sweet Victorian decline, and the twilight of whose decadence was the Edwardian fragment then but barely broken off.

Many years later, when the War was nearly over, Farrer, meditating upon the "inextinguishable lamps of God amid the disasters that man has made of his life", was moved to one of his more richly sombre passages of prose:

"This is no idle fantasy: little happinesses may look little, and find no place in the plans of diplomats and prophets; but these outlast the worst catastrophes and survive the plans and the diplomats and the prophets and all. Dead bones in their grave lie Mary and Elizabeth, Queens; and dead dust of death is all they did; but the flowers that grew in their gardens still continue giving comfort and delight perpetually, down through the continuing generations, to whom the people of the past are mere phantasmal fictions in books, diaphanous, desiccated as dried flowers themselves. All the wars of the world, all the Caesars have not the staying power of a Lily in a cottage border: man creates the storms in his teacup, and dies of them, but there remains a something standing outside, a something impregnable, as far beyond reach of man's destructiveness as is man's own self. The immortality of marbles and of miseries is a vain, small thing compared to the immortality of a flower that blooms and is dead by dusk."

Let us pray that he was not over-sanguine. At least the atomic bomb that extinguished Hiroshima caused the local flora to flourish.

When news of the War did at last reach them they supposed, like most people, that it would soon be over—thinking, perhaps, that it was not much more serious than the local Chinese affairs they were becoming accustomed to. There seemed no cause for any alteration of plans. In November they brought to a close the activities of a year—a year that Farrer called "*Annus Mirabilis*" —by settling down to winter quarters in the Chinese town of Lanchow.

There they remained, reading six-weeks-old newspapers. And thence they emerged again towards the end of March when they reckoned that spring would once more have melted the mountains.

The second year's collecting was no less adventurous than the first, and in point of plants it was even more important. It saw the discovery of *Gentiana Farreri*, his most famous addition to the flora of European gardens, and of many other only less valuable flowers. As for adventures, they were numerous and unexpected and they occur with intelligent artistry in the narrative. A simple short cut becomes, not so much a long way round as a long way down:

> "But now there was no more to do but saunter leisurely round the corner, and up to Tien Tang. I sauntered, I came to the corner, I came round it.
> "I saw nothing before me any more but a blank bare wall of rock, far and sheer to the bird's-eyed fury of the Da Tung, darkly roaring below, in its wildest rage, round the bend of the cliff. The path had wholly vanished, and in front there were only more naked precipices, and more beyond, rosy in the fierceness of the sunlight."

He had already accomplished, in fear and trembling, one tricky bit of climbing, and now he found himself

> "between the Devil of a backward descent down that first cliff . . . and the deep sea of that river, roaring

so far down, straight beneath the precipice across which, apparently, I was meant to adhere like a fly. Between the choices I wavered, but Gomer" (his servant) "now came along with his radiant air of everything always being such fun, and ran a little way down that cranny like any cat, and smiled up at me reassuringly. . . . So down I sat, and deliberately began my downward journey over the face of the cliff, from slab to horrible smooth slab of the cranny, with Gomer backing down below me, arranging my feet with nice precision wherever foothold was dimly indicated. Had I worn nails that day, my death it would assuredly have been; as it was, I put the very smallest trust in my boots, and went as nervously as any old maid in a marsh, levering myself down inch by inch on my seat—a method of progression that makes up in security what it undeniably lacks in grandeur. . . ."

And so, gradually and by perilous degrees, to safety. Farrer incurred some dislike among his earlier travelling companions by displaying them in unbecoming or undignified situations. But he was concerned only with the art of story-telling, which here and there needs comic relief, and he was as willing to unleash the Muse of Comedy upon himself as upon any of his friends. An egoist he may have been—certainly was—but not an egoist un-self-aware or un-self-critical.

At the end of the second year, the expedition's original scheme having been completed, Farrer started for home, reaching Peking early in December and England in the spring of 1916. Here he offered himself for military service, but was rejected on medical grounds, and found employment in the Foreign Office. He found time also to deal with the slow progress through the press of his two great volumes on *The English Rock Garden*, which he had been working on during his enforced winter idleness in China. At some time he was sent as a civilian to France and wrote *The Void of War*. The desolate depression of those Western Front battlefields has been described a hundred times. Farrer did not have to endure them, but their sheer ugliness filled him with horror.

> "Not so long since," he writes, "I stood on the levelled land out beyond Ypres; all the world was a flat indiscriminate muddle of raw mud, without a blade of grass or living green thing anywhere as far as eye could stretch in every direction, along the livid leaden lines of the distance, with trees and houses now unguessable, mere blackened splinters and spars of matchwood here and there; and the waste was pitted universally with shellholes like bleared eyes, full of foul water; and the clammy mud oozed horrible colours; and the whole air was sick with a stale vile smell; and all the earth with horrors hidden or revealed. . . ."

His description of these horrors becomes something ghoulish though not morbid. Farrer was prepared to face blank ugliness, though at its worst, even in the Ypres salient, he believed it to be "something local, detachable, evanescent, while beauty is something preponderant, impregnable and eternal".

The War, in fact, left him on the whole unscathed. The moment it was over his mind fled back to his beloved mountains and their precious plants. And where Farrer's mind went his body was apt to follow.

At the end of 1918 he determined to explore the highlands of Upper Burma, and to that botanically little known land he set out with Mr. E. H. M. Cox. This expedition was Farrer's solitary failure. As Mr. Cox says, "The sad truth is that these Burmese hills do not breed species of alpines that give any return for care or kindness at the hands of the gardener."

So disappointing was the district that Mr. Cox came home at the end of the first season. Farrer, however, grumbling and complaining at the plant-poverty, decided to remain on for another year. He was never easily or for long dejected, and his letters to Mr. Cox show him in his usual buoyant spirits. If he could not find flowers of the field, there were yet flowers of speech at the point of his fluent pen. He wrote that he was engaged on a "new masterpiece" to be called *Latter Ends: or a little book of Consolation for Obscure but Respectable people like You and Me.*

Alas, his own latter end was approaching. In the last week of September 1920, with only native helpers, he was collecting such seeds as there were in continuous unrelenting rain. At a place called Nyitadi he fell ill, with a bad cough and pains in his chest. On 14 October he could no longer take any food except soda-water and whiskey. On the 17th, at half past eleven in the morning, he died —"without," as his servants wrote to Mr. Cox, "giving any pain or trouble to us". They carried his body down and buried it above the fort at Konglu. Mr. Cox has given an account of this final plant-hunt in his book, *Farrer's Last Journey*. On a memorial set up to him by his family in the garden at Ingleborough, Farrer is described as "Author, traveller, botanist, and flower-painter". He was also, and pre-eminently, a gardener and a man of rare personality.

In appearance Farrer was plump, rather less than tall, and heavily moustachioed. He did not smoke. Otherwise he looked like anything from a stockbroker to a stone-breaker—which last, of course, he was. He never married, though if one reads rightly between the lines it would appear that he was the rejector and not the rejected in some more than day-dream romance. He had many women friends, beyond those to whom he dedicated his various books. He liked women and claimed that he understood them; and he was an appreciative connoisseur of their novels—from Jane Austen, through Rhoda Broughton, to Amanda McKittrick Ross. He was perhaps the sort of man who might have married late.

But if it comes to that, one does not easily make up one's mind as to the sort of man Farrer was. He is likely to become legendary. No one who knew him was indifferent to him. Always he roused affection or hostility and sometimes both in turn. Reading his books without ever having known him, one sees how easily this could be. There are remembered occasions when he behaved with uncommon inconsideration. On one of his visits to Ireland he was a guest at the house of Sir Frederick Moore, the director of the Royal Botanic Gardens at Glasnevin. At luncheon, the only provision of his hostess that he would eat was one banana. The rest of his meal was eaten from a paper bag on his lap—to the wide-eyed enchantment of a small boy who was present.

Such table manners, however, might be written off as a not-unamiable eccentricity—anyhow, in retrospect. But after lunch Farrer insisted on attending a lecture given by Sir Frederick to a number of botany and horticulture students. At one point in the discourse Farrer interrupted and, in his much-impedimented speech, at length conveyed to the lecturer—his host and a distinguished scientist more than twenty years his senior—that the Latin name of a plant had been rendered with a false quantity. It is difficult to condone such bad manners—more especially as Farrer's views on the pronunciation of plant names were peculiar, pedantic, and by no means impeccable.

Yet, when placed in the balance against his varied and unquestionable genius, perhaps such matters weigh with but a trivial lightness. Let the last word on his character be with the last of his friends to see him:

"His character," says Mr. Cox, "was so intricate that it is impossible to lay down the law and make definite statements. All who knew him well recognized his moods, and, if they were wise, laid their plans accordingly. A year is a long time to be alone with a single companion, but we came through it with flying colours and with our friendship unimpaired."

Reginald Farrer's importance as a gardener is perhaps less difficult to discern.

CHAPTER VI

THE ROCK-GARDEN'S DEBT TO FARRER

THE history of nineteenth-century gardening, or a long stretch of it, can be traced in the many works of Miss Rhoda Broughton—a writer esteemed by Farrer. In her earlier novels, those of the 'sixties, 'seventies, and 'eighties, there are magnificent displays of bedding-out. Later we come to "broad herbaceous borders, where a noble army of michaelmas daisies in their infinite purple gradations, gay chrysanthemums, and gaudier nasturtiums—summer's last Army Corps—were keeping near-scowling winter at bay". And by 1912 Miss Broughton, who, if as a novelist she did not improve with the years, certainly moved with the times, discovers her Elizabeth Delany "in the rock-garden, kneeling on a small mat and inserting minute plants into little 'pockets' of special soil under the shelter of protecting stones".

That was in the autumn, and by next summer "Elizabeth had made herself an immense sunbonnet, in which she knelt for hours beside the rock-garden, with Knot holding her spare implements and doing much serious digging and scuffling for her". These are the earliest purely literary references to rock-gardening that I know of, and they show that by 1912 Farrer's over-flowing enthusiasm was having its full effect. Twenty years later, John Buchan could, without incongruity, invent a conversation on rock-gardens between business men in a railway carriage.

Outside the world of fiction, Farrer had begun to make his indelible mark with the publication of his earliest books. Indeed, by 1914, two years after Miss Broughton's last novel was written, rock-gardening seemed to be getting out of hand.

> "Now," wrote Farrer, "everyone must have their 'rock-work', and the very rich are out to purchase the glories of the alps at so much a yard—with all the more contentment if the price is heavy, so that their munificence may be the more admired."

You cannot, unfortunately, have popularity without having also some vulgarity. Farrer's vivacious writing was the major cause of the one, the sole cause of the other was innate bad taste in certain rich gardeners.

Apart from a general propaganda which infused and enthused a new life into rock-gardening, Farrer per-formed three particular services for rock-gardeners. In the first place, of the vast number of plants that he collected and introduced to cultivation, the great majority were "alpines" of the type best suited by planting among rocks. Secondly, he popularised if he did not actually invent the "moraine" or "scree" garden. Finally, in the two bulky but not ponderous volumes of *The English*

Rock Garden, he produced a classic and quite indispensable work of reference.

Of his botanical discoveries Mr. Cox has written a full account called *The Plant Introductions of Reginald Farrer*, illustrated from Farrer's own exact and sensitive paintings. His new species and varieties—new, that is, to science—run into hundreds. And there are many others that were previously known and named, but which he was the first to bring into cultivation.

Not counting his finds on his native Ingleborough, such as *Arenaria gothica*, new to these islands, and the natural hybrid *Saxifraga Farreri*, the earliest of his well-known introductions was the beautiful and distinctive variety of the all-too-variable *Saxifraga aeizoon* which he called "Rex". This he discovered in the Alps in 1903 and sent home, as he says, in the same box "that was illustrated by *Campanula Bellardii Miranda*", a plant which "took away the garden's breath" when it bloomed—of a "diaphanous and pale china-blue, like a fine cloud at night with the moon behind it". He called it "Miranda" after one of his many girl-friends, and it has not quite attained the popularity he prophesied for it.

Later, such plants as these were to seem almost commonplace. By far Farrer's most memorable finds were a number of primulas and one famous gentian. The *Primulaceae* were perhaps Farrer's favourite genus. He experimented much in hybridising various European species, and he conveys something of his veneration for the primulas in general when he writes that "a cold awe sweeps across the gardener as he comes at last into the shadow of this grim and glorious name".

Of his discoveries in this genus, *Primula Farreriana*, called after him by Professor Balfour of the Edinburgh Botanic Gardens, was not hardy enough for cultivation in these islands. And this is hardly surprising, for, from the moment of its discovery on the Da Tung Alps in 1915 Farrer recognised that "despite its stalwart growth and size" there was "something ghostly and tragic about its wistful splendour, so Quakerish in its combinations of colour". Nor did better luck befall *Primula reginella*, a name devised for the plant by Farrer himself "in tribute to its own regal but tiny charm, but also to give an *arrière pensée* of its inventor's christian name". This primula seems not now to be in cultivation, though its finder expected it to survive in specially choice and safe-guarded corners of the garden.

Among many new species, Farrer also added one new genus to botanical knowledge when, during the 1914 season, he came upon "a singularly lovely little ground Daphne, with clusters of bright citron-yellow flowers". This plant, of which he could get neither seed nor roots, was named from dried specimens *Farreria pretiosa*.

The next year, however, provided him with his greatest glory—*Gentiana Farreri*. He describes its discovery in *The Rainbow Bridge*. He was returning to his camp across a mountain crest:

> "Hardly had I started when, in the fine turf that crowned the top of a sloping boulder, there stared at me a new Gentian, a Gentian that instantly obliterate all others of its race, and sinks even *G. Verna* and *G. Gentianella* into a common depth of dullness. When the first awe was over, I gave tongue for Bill, and together, in reverend silence, we contemplated that marvel of luminous loveliness."

Such was his excitement that for once Farrer's sense of words failed him—he wrote species names with capital letters, he wrote "rever*end*" when he meant "rever*ent*", and he was guilty—oh, horror!—of "giving tongue". But one cannot blame him, for, as he went on when he had pulled himself together:

"The collector's dream is to have some illustrious plant to bear his name immortal through the gardens of future generations, long after he himself shall have become dust of their paths. Mere beauty will not do; for the plant may fail and fade in cultivation, and his name be no more known, except to the learned, as attached to a dead dry sliver on the sheets of a herbarium. To become vividly immortal in the Valhalla of gardeners, one must own a species as vigorous as it is glorious, a thing capable of becoming and remaining a household word among English enthusiasts."

And certainly, in *Gentiana Farreri* the collector's dream came true—or very nearly. We have all admired it, and most of us have grown it—though I myself have for some reason never been able to keep it for very long; but then, even my *gentianellas* will flower from their great mats only sparsely and at the wrong season—and if Farrer's ecstasies seem the least bit excessive, that is not to be wondered at. And *Gentiana Farreri* would keep his name alive, even if there were nothing else to help it.

This gentian was certainly the high watermark of his achievement. He found other notable plants—the silver geranium, *Geranium Farreri* which has gained an Award of Merit from the Royal Horticultural Society; *Isopyrum Farreri*, *Trollius Farreri*, and many more; and he was the first European to discover *Viburnum fragrans* growing as a wild plant, though it had long been grown in all the gardens of China. But none of these confer the fame of his brilliant gentian.

And of course Farrer's reputation is not founded on his gentian alone, nor on all his plant introductions put together. As a practical gardener his name is most notably connected with what he called the "moraine".

In his book called *In a Yorkshire Garden*, Farrer describes briefly the making of his first moraine:

> "Four big blocks of beautifully worn limestone were arranged in a hollow square, with a well at their centre. Some sharp, large rubbish was put in for drainage, and then the whole filled in with chips of blue limestone, such as they use in these parts for mending the roads. And with this a faint adulteration, only, of soil."

According to the dictionary, the word "moraine" means "an accumulation of débris from the mountains carried down and deposited by a glacier", which is not exactly the formation described by Farrer. The word has therefore been replaced in garden usage by the ugly monosyllable "scree", defined by the dictionary as "a mass of detritus, forming a precipitous, stony slope upon a mountain side", which is supposed in some way to come nearer to Farrer's fact. In any case, the name is not important. The point is that in this extremely lean mixture —stone chippings with but a minimum of loam or leaf-mould—Farrer found that he could grow, maintain in health, and even increase, many high alpines that consistently failed under all other forms of treatment.

It seems certain that Farrer discovered the "moraine" for himself. But it seems equally certain that others had discovered it, or something very like it, before him. A certain Robert Mallet, presumably a relative of the famous engineer, writing to the *Gardener's Magazine* in August 1832, tells how he kept ninety-seven species of mesembryanthemum out of doors all the year round in his garden at Drumcondra north of Dublin: "The mesembryanthemums are on rockwork with interstices filled with pebbles and a little earth, and are growing luxuriantly." Farrer's friend, Mr. E. A. Bowles, gives a short moraine history in his book, *My Garden in Spring*:

"I suppose it is inevitable," says Mr. Bowles, "that I write of my moraines. . . . No one would read a gardening book nowadays that did not deal with this latest fashion in gardening. The name and popularity and prattle of the thing are new, but many good cultivators had their porous, gritty, raised or sunk beds for alpines, whatever they called them, long ago. Mr. Wooley-Dod laughingly called his narrow raised mounds 'potato-ridges'. But they proved the ideal home for many difficult plants that would not exist domiciled otherwise on the cold, sticky clay of Edge Hill. The ridges were, as I remember them, about twenty yards long, and mainly composed of grit and leaf-soil, and ever full of rare and healthy plants. The ridge system was the important factor of success at Edge, but in the hungry, arid, gravel soil at Cambridge, Mr. Lynch found a sunk bed of gritty soil made a happy home for Saxifrages that repined and went into a decline under other treatment. Then arose the prophet. The abundant rainfall of Ingleborough and the local limestone . . . aided and abetted by river silt from the lake's mouth and chips of all sizes from the mountain side, were only waiting for Mr. Farrer's master mind to plan their combination and lo! a new era dawned."

Mr. Bowles was writing in 1913. It is perfectly true that gardeners had for years—for about a hundred years, in fact—been growing alpines on "raised beds". One need look no further than Loudon to find this method of growing them recommended. But neither Loudon's raised beds nor Mr. Wooley-Dod's "potato-ridges" were a "moraine" as Farrer understood the word, though probably they performed the same sort of function. But leaving the question of priority aside, and it has been over-laboured by some people, there can be no doubt that the wave of enthusiasm for moraine gardening just before the First World War was entirely owing to Farrer. It had become a craze. It had, according to Mr. Bowles, become the staple of polite dinner-table conversation.

The success of the moraine or scree garden depends on two factors: paucity of soil and perfect drainage. For the rock-garden in general, drainage was the main material point on which Farrer insisted. It was the text of all his preaching, and its supreme importance was everywhere conceded. Rock-gardens, however, are not merely material media for the growing of certain plants —though that must be their primary object—and Farrer was at least as much concerned with the garden's spiritual and aesthetic aspects.

Here his uncompromising views, vigorously and wittily expressed, led him into fairly frequent controversy. He classified various rock-gardens he disapproved of into several satiric types—as the Almond-pudding, the Plum-bun, the Dog's Grave, the Drunkard's Dream, and the Devil's Lap-full. To this last kind he considered that the rock-work in the Botanic Garden at Glasnevin belonged, though he had to concede to that fine garden an ability to grow more rare plants and grow them better than most.

Other gardeners were less urbane or more touchy than the Director of Glasnevin. In 1912 Farrer wrote a small book for the *Present Day Gardening* series edited by Professor Bretland Farmer. In this book, because it was written as a link in a popular chain, Farrer rather tempered and toned down his provocative approach. None the less, he fell foul of William Robinson who, in one of his crossest moods, reviewed the book in *Gardening Illustrated*.

What irritated Robinson was "the black and white illustrations—one can hardly call them drawings—which the author supplies at pages 8 and 9". Robinson thought these illustrations "such as one might send to a cheap comic paper to ridicule the subject". "Indeed," he goes on, "we are not quite sure whether the author is not poking fun at his readers." Robinson's sense of fun was ever an uncertain quantity, especially when he was irritated, and Farrer's very funny drawings had certainly irritated him. And there was worse to come.

In the middle of the book Farrer requested, instructed, his readers that when they were talking of Saxifrages they should "conspue that detestable affectation of 'Rockfoil': plain 'Saxifrage' is quite as good English as anyone could want". This contemptuous direction drove Robinson to incoherent frenzy, for was it not the idolised Ruskin who had, from the purest motives, invented the name Rock Foil?

"We are quite sure," said Robinson, "we are quite sure that, after all these little ephemera of the day, including Mr. Farrer's own books, the Proserpina of Mr. Ruskin will be alive and well. The division of Saxifraga into sub-sections with ugly Latin names is no gain, all the more so when the author drops into the habit of using these instead of Saxifraga. . . . Think of the British maiden or her mother struggling with such pedantic ugliness."

Robinson's meaning is a shade obscure, but from the last sentence his motive appears as pure as Ruskin's own.

Farrer's reply was restrained and good-tempered, for Robinson was even then old, and the two had been on friendly terms when Farrer contributed to Robinson's *Flora and Sylva*:

> "I am sorry," he wrote, "that my poor little book seems to have rather annoyed you. At the same time let us be fair. I did not invent the subdivisions of Saxifraga, but merely adopted Engler's very simple and luminous classification. . . . I cannot believe that any matron or maid could be silly enough to boggle over so clear a matter. If, however, they are, obviously one does not write even small botanical guide-books for the assistance of idiots, and I can appeal quite comfortably to the more sensible millions. With regard to Mr. Ruskin, do you then claim that he stands beyond reach of all human criticism? . . . Of doubtful mental balance through most of his life, and quite off it in later years, Mr. Ruskin combines, with a great quantity of glorious and valuable work, no less a quantity, surely, of fustian and foolishness? Therefore I repeat . . . that he made a small but signal blunder of taste in trying to replace a sound, euphonious, easy, and significant name like 'saxifrage' by the cheap and gratuitous Anglo-French affectation of 'Rock Foil'."

After a few more gentle prods by way of Ruskin at the presumably writhing Robinson, he turns to the question of his illustrations:

> "I wish I could have made my drawings plainer. I had not imagined that anyone could fail to see that

they were caricatures, but alas! in so small and cheap
a book one has not the resources that were able to give
such delicious point to those exquisite parodies that
appear, for instance, in *The Rock Garden.*"

The last-named book was, of course, Robinson's own
volume of 1870.

Farrer's reply to Robinson might easily have been
more damaging, but it was decisive enough. Of his other
controversies, at least one was of some interest, though it
was curiously one-sided. In 1914 Messrs. Jack issued the
first volume in a series under the general direction of
R. Hooper Pearson, a friend of Farrer's and at that time
editor of the *Gardener's Chronicle.* This volume was the
well-known and by now hard to come by book of Mr.
E. A. Bowles, called *My Garden in Spring.* Mr. Bowles was
also a friend of Farrer; and Farrer was induced either by
the author or the editor to provide a nine-page preface
to the book. The preface is in Farrer's most nimbly satiric
manner. He describes and pokes fun at, without actually
naming, the notorious rock-garden manufactured at Friar
Park near Henley by Sir Frank Crisp—a solicitor whose
recreations were Company Law, Horticulture, and
Microscopy, in that order.

The Friar Park garden, in its ostentatious extravagance, was one of the show places of the period. It was of
vast size, containing caves and ice-grottoes and a Matter-
horn done in slate and concrete, with herds of tin chamois
peeping among the cement rocks. No doubt it was all a
wonder and a wild desire, but, as Farrer said, why call
it a *garden*? In this same preface, Farrer not unnaturally
praised Mr. Bowles's garden as being, what it was, the
very opposite of Sir Frank Crisp's.

But, though the preface had serious undertones, its
surface tone was lighthearted enough; and in places

Farrer's ridicule is even turned good-naturedly against
Bowles himself. And no other person or place is mentioned by name.

However, such was Farrer's prestige as an arbiter of
gardening taste, that Crisp considered both his own
reputation and that of his monstrous rockery to have been
seriously mangled. Still, Crisp would probably have let
the matter go if it had not happened that at exactly this
time his friend, that enigmatic character but unquestion-
ably great gardener, Miss Ellen Willmott, was nursing a
private grudge against Mr. Bowles. That being so, there
followed a Willmott-Crisp alliance the outcome of which
was an eight-page quarto pamphlet with the title *Mr.
E. A. Bowles and his Garden* and the sub-title, *A New
Parable of the Pharisee and the Publican.* In it the Friar Park
garden was defended and Mr. Bowles was attacked with a
recklessly unscrupulous spite worthy of the scurrilous
pamphlet wars of the seventeenth or eighteenth centuries.

The preface to Mr. Bowles's book is quoted, first in
its denigration of the kind of gardening enjoyed at Friar
Park and then in praise of Mr. Bowles's own garden, and
the preface as a whole and each quotation from it in
particular is tacitly attributed to Mr. Bowles himself. With
an air of self-righteous indignation these passages are held
up to the reader as examples of ungentlemanly criticism
and conceited self-praise. There is not the slightest
suggestion that the passages quoted, each and all of them,
were from the impish pen of Reginald Farrer. Had Miss
Willmott—for there is no doubt that she was mainly
responsible—allowed it to be known that she was quoting
Farrer and not Bowles, the pamphlet's pretensions would
have vanished in air.

As it is, the pamphlet reaches its lowest ebb in a
footnote on the second page where a "special pique" is
attributed to Mr. Bowles "in that we declined an offer

from the writer to buy for £250 (!) a plant of *Daphne rupestris*, and added to our offence by not responding to other invitations that equally did not appeal to us". A statement no less studiedly ambiguous than intentionally offensive, and, whatever its meaning, almost certainly untrue. For, if Miss Willmott wished to convey that "the writer" offered to *buy* Crisp's *Daphne*, the suggestion is unlikely since Farrer had at the time a very famous bush of *Daphne rupestris* which never failed to blossom exactly in time for the Royal Horticultural Society's summer show—no matter how the date varied.

"The flowers open the day before the show," wrote Farrer in 1918, "and the nervous tension is such that they all drop off the day after it is over." And he had had that plant for twelve years. Nor is the suggestion that he tried to *sell* his plant any more likely, since he had many times refused to sell it. And if by chance the statement was really aimed at Mr. Bowles, it is even more patently improbable, since, in this very book, *My Garden in Spring*, he explains that his poverty prevents him from growing the more fashionable kinds of Daffodil. Besides, Miss Willmott was not notorious for strict accuracy.

The pamphlet then goes on to marshal a cloud of witnesses for the defence of Friar Park—witnesses who ranged from an anonymous (and quite irrelevant) newspaper-writer, to "His Imperial Highness the Archduke Francis Ferdinand, Crown Prince of Austria".

Having compiled and printed this surprising document, Miss Willmott repaired to the entrance gate of the Royal Horticultural Society's summer show, where she stood, handing copies to all comers from a bookmaker's large leather bag.

Fortunately—or perhaps unfortunately—Farrer, on that particular date, was flower-gathering in the mountain fastness of Tibet. And by the time he was again in

England a more-than-horticultural war was raging over
the dead body of "His Imperial Highness the Archduke
Francis Ferdinand, Crown Prince of Austria". Had it
been otherwise, Farrer would certainly have enjoyed
himself, for he was not one to leave any stone un-
returned, and in elegant vituperation he was more than
a match for his traducers—as they were probably well
aware.

Beyond its mere gossip-value in connexion with Farrer,
this odd incident is relevant as underlining Farrer's
gardening ideas. Sir Frank Crisp's rock-garden—now
gone, with so many other great gardens—was, while it
lasted, of the "Drunkard's Dream" type, and it offended
against all the canons that Farrer was, fairly successfully,
trying to establish. Like Pope and Shenstone, like Repton
and Loudon, like Robinson and Miss Jekyll, Farrer was a
propagandist prophet in the name of Nature. Like them,
he interpreted Nature partly in the light of observation,
and partly in the rich shadow of his own prejudice.
"Nature," he preached, "is never haphazard: inspira-
tions from nature must never be haphazard either. Never
think you are going to get a dignified result by humping
a quantity of stones indiscriminately together." So—
Nature must be orderly, Nature must be dignified, never,
never "humping a quantity of stones indiscriminately
together". Mr. Farrer has said so.

But heavens, one has only to look at the confusion of
rock fragments, the higgledy-piggledy chaos that is a
true glacial moraine—indeed, one need only look at the
photographs in some of Farrer's own books—to see how
Nature really behaves when she is dealing with stones:
and, what is more, how plants grow amongst them.
The fact is, naturally, that Nature often is, by human
standards, a perfect slut, and one might as well admit it.
But then, having admitted what is so obvious, let us agree

with Farrer or anyone else that there is no reason, no excuse, for imitating Nature in her more slatternly moods and modes.

Farrer's prejudice appears again when he is discussing the kind of stone suitable for a rock-garden. One agrees that "no brick, no slag, no clinkers, no fragments of masonry or statues" should be used—or not visibly used. One may go further, and agree that the white mountain limestone of Yorkshire is far and away the best. One begins to doubt, however, when he is indiscriminately disrespectful about sandstone. And one stops agreeing altogether when he says that "granite is only to be used as a resource of despair". Farrer had an irrational dislike of granite. "This stone has never had any part in life; life passes it by, receiving no companionship, and giving none," he said—speaking pure nonsense. His hatred of granite may have come from his disappointment in trying to grow those numerous and beautiful alpines that will not grow on anything else, demanding an acid soil, and quietly dying with a hint of lime.

It is not so easy to garden in granite, but it can be done. The best of the rock-gardens that I know at all well is in nothing but granite. And my own rock-garden, though it is lamentably far from perfection or even excellence, is made in a re-excavated granite quarry, the face of which is ragged and sharp as the eighteenth-century quarry-men left it. But on top and on the gentler slopes, where the surface soil has been removed, the granite shows itself eroded into curves by the last glacier of the great Ice Age, and washed into fissures by all the rains that have fallen since.

It is perfectly true that where one is not working with virgin rock or with very large boulders, granite is difficult to build up with. It has no stratification, and it does not weather quickly. Also it has an angular fracture.

Parts of my garden are still rather of Farrer's Almond-pudding variety; but they will not always be so, when their plants are well grown.

Farrer's positive advice is, in fact, nearly always sound. It is mainly his too-sweeping negations that need qualifying or contradicting. And this is not surprising. Inevitably the scope of his advice was limited by the conditions best known to him. His own successes were obtained with a mountain limestone of uncommon charm, and his garden included a fine natural cliff of which he said that it was the most wholly rewarding and beautiful of all his territories. Also, at first anyhow, he was obliged to rely solely on his own experience.

In the matter of rock-garden construction he was far more of a pioneer than he is generally given credit for. The English rock-garden is of ancient but unpromising lineage. It descends from the eighteenth-century grotto which came from Italy and from which we get the appropriate word "grotesque". And ideally the grotto was a sort of museum conglomerate of every kind of hard substance—coloured marble, spa, flints, shells, skulls, old statuary, mirror-glass—amongst which, perhaps accidentally at first, a few ferns would grow. The eighteenth century also devised a somewhat similar structure called the "Root-house", a wildly Gothic arrangement of old tree-stumps and, if possible, whale-bones. The root-house was in-tended to grow ferns.

At the beginning of the nineteenth century the rockery, including tree-stumps, was nearly always a fernery. The fernery tradition—dampness with a north aspect—continued long after a genuine interest in alpine plants had been aroused and maintained by such garden experts as Jane Loudon and by nurserymen like the firm of Backhouse at York. In 1870 William Robinson pub-lished his little book on the growing of alpines, but

Robinson's chief interest was in herbaceous plants, and his writing on rock-gardens lacks emphasis. So it happened that, one way or another, the whole field was there, not for Farrer to discover, but for Farrer to explore. It was certainly he and none other that created the interest, the enthusiasm, the rage, for rock-gardening as a separate branch of horticulture.

This enthusiasm was aroused by Farrer's early book, *My Rock Garden*. It was increased by many other similar books and essays. And then in 1919 came his great, his monumental, contribution to garden literature, the two volumes—more than a thousand pages—of *The English Rock Garden*.

It is hard to write temperately of *The English Rock Garden*. Some people detest it, whilst admitting its great usefulness. To an increasing number of others it is, in spite of its weight, a favourite bedside book; and to these the temptation is not to write about it but to make from it multitudinous quotations, creating for once an almost unmetaphorical anthology.

No matter which party one belongs to, no one will question that Farrer's long, long-winded work is unique. Where would you look to find a professional treatise which was so obviously also a work of literary art—even if the art is inappropriate? Mr. Edmund Blunden has praised William Ellis's *Complete System of Experienced Improvements Made on Sheep*, for its style; and Sir Charles Lyell's prose was uncommonly good in his *Principles of Geology*. But such books are not really comparable. Their writers wrote well by the light of their age and by the rare lucidity of their mind and eye. And also, their books are not true technical books as we now think of such things. Whoever heard of a learned discourse on drainage construction or dentistry or the internal-combustion engine that could be read with enjoyment for its own

THE ROCK-GARDEN'S DEBT TO FARRER   157

sake? Nor will gardening literature itself provide another
example.

Yet here was an expert, a professional, addressing his
colleagues, expounding his subject from A to Z—for the
book is, in form, a dictionary—giving first-hand information on a limited range of plants, and on far more plants
within that range than any one reader is likely to meet in
a long gardening life, and writing of these plants and their
culture not only as a horticultural expert but as an artist
in words: writing of them as De Quincy might write of a
dream, as Pater might write of the Mona Lisa, with the
rhetoric of Burke remembering the Queen of France. No
wonder a horny-handed Fellow of the Royal Horticultural
Society, turning these pages in a hurry, finds them
disconcerting, mutters, perhaps, "It is magnificent, but
it is not the gardening," and, exasperated, swears he will
in future get his information elsewhere. But he will not,
or hardly.

If one wants to know what difference, if any, lies
between *Hyacinthus azureus* and *Hyacinthus ciliatus*, one will
in time find out—after one has been entangled in much
magnificence, been taken back, as one might expect, into
classical mythology, and been introduced, more surprisingly, to a minor modern novelist:

> "Hyacinthus—Of this race there are many children,
> but the head of all is *Hyacinthus orientalis*, the delicate
> and lovely Lear of all the terrible mondaine (or
> elderly demi-mondaine) Hyacinths, immense frizzed
> women of the world, scented and unctuous and rather
> stolidly complacent, that decorate every home in
> spring. Yet even these, in time, like Hall Caine's
> heroines who wax fat on urban vice for a while and
> then remember the paternal farm, and go back there
> to recover virtue on a diet of milk, will eventually,

after a year or two of prostitution in pots, remember
Hyacinth and the favour of the sun, and will even
grow worthy of the rock-garden if put in some deep
warm corner, where their stems will become slenderer
with repentance every season and their blossoms
renew the untarnished purity of their innocence."

But with patience one will find what one set out to find
—if one still remembers what it was.

But again, how one will be led astray, Who would not
seek through catalogues for the Oncocyclus Irids, having
been told that

"They are a doomed and lonely race of irreconcil-
able Troades in weeds of silken crape, sullenly and
grandly unresigned to exile and captivity, passing out
of their captor's hands in a last defiant blaze of dark
and tragic magnificence. They are chief mourners in
their own funeral pomps, wistful and sombre and
royal in an unearthly beauty of their own, native to
the Syrian hills that have seen the birth of gods,
but strange and hostile to the cruder colder lands.
They are the maidens that went down into hell with
Persephone, and yearly in her train they return to
make a carpet for her feet across the limestones of
the Levant. But not for ours—their loyalty to their
mistress holds only good in Syria; they do not recognize
her in the raincloaks that she wears in the West, and
lands of younger divinities shall never twice re-greet
such children of mystery as these."

In other words, but who would substitute those other
words, the Oncocyclus Irids may survive in your garden
for one season but not for two. Meantime, you have been
fired with a hopeless passion for an Oncocyclus Iris.

Yet the practical stuff, born of personal experience, is all there too. *Dianthus neglectus* "is a plant, in nature, obviously lime-hating, but not so completely so as *D. glacialis*. Get it into poorish deep soil in full sun, and its massive circles will yearly increase, and with them will increase the profusion of its blossom." Still, if in these volumes there is much to be learned if you want to find out about flowers, in finding it out you will, willy-nilly, find out much also about Farrer. And that being so, it would seem as well to take an interest in him.

As a small sample, consider the article on *Sedum album*. In the course of it, not a long course and after calling it a typical weed of the race, he goes on: "Within a year of receiving two squashed sprigs in a letter, you will be casting it out of your garden in cartloads. . . . It is as hard to get rid of as love or lime." From such a hint, in conjunction with the themes of his novels, is one justified, however impertinently, in guessing at something like a Samuel Butlerish love-affair? Was *Sedum album* somehow connected with the "dear dear Sophia of my heart" once so unexpectedly invoked "among the hills"? Perhaps not. But it is Farrer's fault if one is tempted to speculate.

In any case, love-affair or no love-affair, *Sedum album* was not one of Farrer's favourite plants. Bees like it and it is worth growing for them, but otherwise no one, heart-free or heart-entangled, would carry it much in memory. Some of his preferences, however, amounted to plain prejudice, and from time to time he honestly tried to counteract their effect. He certainly aspired to a liberal humility in the cause of his craft.

"I think the true gardener," he said in one of these moods, "is a lover of his flowers, not a critic of them. I think the true gardener is the reverent

> servant of Nature, not her truculent, wife-beating master. I think the true gardener, the older he grows, should more and more develop a humble, grateful and uncertain spirit."

In a final analysis, supposing such a thing possible of any man, that spirit—humble, grateful, and uncertain—would surely be found at the core of his humorously egoistical temperament. It could hardly be otherwise, creating the garden that he did, where "the winds sweep icy down from the North, and incessant Ingleborough deluges descend without mitigation": since, in fact, he was an Englishman ceaselessly contending for his flowers with the characteristic climate of these islands.

I have counted Farrer as a nineteenth-century gardener not only because half his life and his earliest gardening activities belong to that century, but also because most of his gardening, writing, collecting—alas, most of his living—were done before the menacing cracks in our civilisation had much appeared over the horizon; when it was still possible to look down vista'd years of the future as complacently as down a Victorian avenue.

As a man he is difficult to place—and one cannot ignore him as a man. As a gardener he was great and original in the great nineteenth-century tradition. Yet also, since one may grow a rock-garden on one's window-sill, he was not less a prophet for our own more uncertain and flat-loving if not flatter age.

The fate of Farrer's garden is the fate of many great gardens. On the death of his younger brother, Mr. Sydney Farrer, early in 1947, the house and grounds at Ingleborough passed to the West Riding County Council as a home for backward children.

CHAPTER VII

BRIEF RETROSPECT

JOHN CLAUDIUS LOUDON, in that he was a Whig, may have believed that education would eliminate our stone-throwing tendencies. He saw no limit to the beneficent use of glasshouses—hardly any limit to their physical extension. Had he lived a few years longer, he would have greeted the Crystal Palace as a small but natural step along the road which he himself had mapped, along the road of progress.

Progress was the watchword of the nineteenth century, or so they supposed who lived at its higher levels. It was the dominant concept in an age of Liberal expansion. Few Englishmen doubted its reality, though William Robinson, for instance, saw that others might be sadly wrong as to its direction. Only after the age was, properly speaking, over, did Reginald Farrer, for all that he remained a nominal Liberal, introduce a sceptical note by writing the word "progress" in inverted commas.

Looking back now at that opulent golden time, its

L

crowded interiors rather stuffily upholstered but with their windows opening on to long-shadowed lawns and letting in "the moan of doves from immemorial elms and murmur of innumerable bees", looking back, not without envy, we can see that, whatever the watchword or the catchword may have been, the keyword was Security.

The Victorians themselves did not worry about security, they took it for granted. Progress is, theoretically, conceivable without it; and, what with Darwin, they might have so conceived it. But progress on insecure terms was not acceptable. One might perspire softly, one should not sweat, and to bleed was unthinkable. Darwin made progress certain; Tennyson gave assurance of its quiet inevitable gradualness. And for Tennyson's Progress, Security was essential. The steam-plough was part of Loudon's picture, but not the aeroplane.

Their sense of security shows itself everywhere. Men built solid houses of brick and stone, they laid down cellars of the best vintage, they bought enormous pictures as an investment, and, in many-volumed editions, the books of writers they did not read. Above all, secure in their finances, they entailed their landed estates.

It was this security of property, and particularly of landed property, that conditioned many of the gardening trends and fashions of the period. People planted trees. They planted hardwood trees. And when, as they often did, they planted conifers, they made a Pinetum, a collection of specimens—not expecting a monetary return in ten years, but in the faith that if they themselves did not live to hear the full beauty of their trees admired, yet their sons and their sons' sons would have that pleasure. Loudon was a tree-planter, Robinson was a tree-planter. Since Robinson's day we have planted shrubs. Tree-planting is left to a Forestry Department which must be prepared for the sake of revenue to ruin the Lake District.

Again, Loudon and Robinson laid out their gardens with a wide gesture on the grand scale. They were landscape gardeners in their conscious aims and in the common sense of the word. And even Farrer had many acres to play with and was aware of prospects—though the growing of an Androsace did not demand them. It was the age of the spacious, the solid, the traditional, even in the smaller gardens. And if it was also—let us preserve a proper perspective—the age of the aspidistra and of many worse things, they need not concern us.

In such a century of stability, gardening history is naturally bound up not only with individuals but with families, Duke after Duke of Devonshire, long lines of Aclands; and also with generations of nurserymen like the Veitches and the Riverses. And it is bound up with great gardens where there was a gradual change within a general continuity, a slow movement from hot-house pine-apples to hardy primulas; and all that such a shifting of emphasis implies. And of those great gardens— Chatsworth, Killerton, Stowe, Ashridge, Knole, Penshurst, Wilton, Longleat, Gravetye: the list could be endless— how many are now in private hands? And is there any reason to expect that public ownership will in future result at least in less philistine neglect than is visible today at Gravetye?

Yet individual gardeners were important. They were more important, more influential, then than the same men would be now. Loudon's influence, the gardening medium being so ephemeral, is not as easily traced as Robinson's; yet the fact that Robinson himself edited one of Loudon's larger books a quarter-century after its author's death, shows that he was not soon eclipsed. Robinson, who perceptibly altered the face of England, was immensely important. And so in his narrower field was Farrer.

There were others, many others, hardly less in stature. Paxton, of course. But Paxton, great gardener in a way though he was, is somehow an unsympathetic figure. He must be the only professional gardener whose gardening has brought him a knighthood—for the Crystal Palace rose directly from the Chatsworth Conservatory—and having become Sir Joseph Paxton he preferred to call himself an Architect. And there are scores of other men. And as for the women—if they were less numerous they were hardly less eminent, from Jane Loudon to Ellen Willmott.

Miss Willmott was as enigmatic and fascinating a character as one could wish to find. She was an ardent Roman Catholic, a lutanist, and one of the founders of the Madrigal Society; she was a woman of great beauty and great pride, travelling always with a retinue and commanding homage; she was quarrelsome and unscrupulous in her quarrelling, the fantastic clouds that began to gather round her in her later years took on a shade almost of tragedy towards her end. Yet when all is said—and as yet it cannot all be said—with her gardens in England, France, and Italy, and her monograph on "The Genus Rosa", not to mention all the plants that bear her name, she stands out as a very great gardener.

Statesmen, soldiers, poets, are all taken account of in history books. Their contributions to our civilisation, to the present sum of our national culture, are recognised; and schoolboys know their names. As a matter of course, their biographies are written within a few years of their death. It is quite otherwise with gardeners; which is curious and surely a little absurd, remembering that Gray, himself a poet, set gardening above poetry as characteristic of the English creative ability. However that may be, gardeners represent a unique aspect of the

English genius. As personalities they are probably above the average in interest, and the mark they have made on the English way of life has been great beyond computation.

At the moment, the outlook for gardening may not seem bright—nor for any other good thing, if it comes to that. But if we have lost the Victorian faith in long-term progress, there is no reason to believe in its long-term opposite. And indeed, even as I write, *The Times* Horticultural Correspondent reports that Gardening enthusiasm tends to be in inverse ratio to Stock Exchange buoyancy. Has every ill wind a silver lining?

NOTE ON NINETEENTH CENTURY
LAWNS AND LAWN-MOWING

FOR the past 200 years and more the lawn has probably been the most constant factor in English gardening. As the gardener's range expanded to the far horizon or contracted to the urban strip; as his enthusiasm turned now towards the glasshouse, now towards the rock-garden; through back-to-nature fashions and fashions of formality—always a lawn of some pretensions, no matter how minute, has entered into every scheme whose ambition rose above that of the allotment. It is our English, Irish, and Scottish lawns that foreigners most envy, and try ineffectually to imitate.

True, there have been dissentient voices—even dissentient English voices. Alice Meynell confessed that she took no delight in lawns, and found even the word itself disagreeable except as used by Tennyson: "The mountain lawn was dewy-dark", or "myriads of rivulets hurrying through the lawn". One feels she must also have liked Arnold's reference to a "wet, bird-haunted English lawn", which more nearly evokes the real thing. But for the actual real thing Mrs. Meynell seems to have had no use. And nor, even more oddly, had that other sensitive writer, W. H. Hudson:

> "I am not a lover of lawns," he said, "rather would I see daisies in their thousands, ground ivy, hawkweed, and even the hated plantain with tall stems, and dandelions with splendid flowers and fairy down, than the too-well-tended lawn."

What, in his perversity, Hudson wanted was a piece of poor pasture, rough and weed-ridden—which, incidentally, was, down to the eighteenth century, one of the common meanings of the word "lawn".

But Hudson and Alice Meynell are exceptional. English poets and English prose-writers too, from the now neglected and, heaven knows, rightly neglected, Vicesimus Knox, to the for ever radiantly to be remembered Francis Bacon, have praised the English lawn without stint.

And so have the foreigners. That good gardener the late Mrs. Earl, recounts with some complacency a fragment of dialogue between two American visitors fifty years ago: "Oh, Jack," said one, "however do they get these lawns here? I can't understand it. *We* can't do it." "Well, my dear," replied her husband, "I guess we can't have the two centuries of mowing which these places have had."

A climate such as that of these islands is, of course, a preliminary good fortune; nor are 200 years of mowing necessary; none the less, mowing is the main essential in maintaining a lawn; and a lawn for playing tennis on must have the mower run over it two or three times a week during the season.

Yet that, to us, indispensable instrument the mechani-

cal lawn-mower, without which there would have been
no centre court at Wimbledon, preceded the invention
of lawn-tennis by well under half a century. And in
those years, so averse from change are lawn-lovers, the
mowing-machine made curiously slow progress. For
several decades most lawns continued to be cut by the
ancient and traditional scythe.

Scything a hayfield is not particularly easy. The
proper scything of a lawn was a performance nearly as
highly skilled as, say, thatching. Robert Thompson, head
gardener to the Royal Horticultural Society, writing in
1859, said that "nothing but a considerable amount of
practice will make a man a good mower of lawns", and
he goes on to give detailed instructions as to how the
scythe should be held and the cut made.

And then, when the mowing itself was done, since
no one ever invented a grass-box attachment for a scythe,
there was the additional labour of collecting the cut
grass, Loudon, who liked such problems, worked out with
mathematical precision the best method of gathering up
lawn-mowings:

"For the cleaning of a lawn after a morning's
mowing," he wrote, "every alternate swarth is to be
raked with a common hayrake in such a way as to
leave a breadth of two swarths for the long-handled
besom. Along the centre of this cleared space, a man
starts with a flattened besom on the end of a nine-foot
handle, and sends all the grass he meets with right
and left, leaving these two swarths cleanly swept. A
boy or a woman, with a short-handled besom, follows
after, and sweeps ten yards of this ridge upward,
and ten yards downward, thus leaving the lawn
studded with heaps of grass sixty feet apart one way,
and fifteen or eighteen feet apart the other way. This

Gentleman pushing one of Edwin Budding's machines,
from *The Gardener's Magazine,* 1832

is again basketed into the grass-cart by a man and a boy with a couple of boards and a besom.

"When this plan is followed," continues Loudon, "all is regularity; the long-handled besom, doing the bulk of the brushing without ever having to touch a blade of grass twice over, is a manly straightforward sweeper; for the person stands upright as a dart, and moves forward in a line, swinging his arms on even balance, furrowing the greensward, whilst the women and boys with their four-foot besoms lay it in heaps."

One can see that Loudon made the best of this laborious process, not only studying how to reduce the actual toil, but turning it into an aesthetic, almost a moral, exercise.

Yet there was one respect in which the gardeners of those days saved a certain amount of time and trouble. With so much in the way of mown grass being swept and carted from the lawns, our forefathers never thought of putting anything back by way of manure. Nor did they bother much about weeds. They wanted a closely cut green surface. And as for manures, in spite of advertise-ments, and though blood and bones and buried Caesars are up to a point good for any lawn—still, when all is said, the best fertilisers are wet and worms.

Worms cultivate the soil to an incredible extent, passing—so Darwin calculated—ten tons of it through their bodies in every acre every year. Which explains, perhaps, why those who offer us patent lawn-manures also offer us patent worm-killers, for without worms well might our lawns deteriorate. Apart from this, one must remember that the great bulk of lawn-mowings removed to the compost heap is not all derived from the soil. Much of the matter in a blade of grass is compiled by sunlight from chemicals in the air. An occasional mowing without the grass-box will put back all that is needed.

However, this not troubling about manures was but a small gain when set against all that scything, raking, brushing, and carting. And it was by some such elaborate process that, from Elizabethan times at least, the beauty of English lawns, many square miles of them, had been maintained. The only alternative instrument was the garden shears. Loudon's own lawn at Bayswater was cut with shears, because of the quantity of bulbs he grew in it. No one for any other reason would willingly cut a lawn with shears.

There was, too, another inconvenience about scything. Lawns could only be scythed when the grass was wet. At Versailles, where the French kings pertinaciously aspired to a lawn, the royal gardeners had to mow what grass there was by moonlight or by torchlight, whilst it was still damp with dew. Even in England this necessity required that mowers must be up early. Such a call for working in the wet had about it, to Loudon's humane and liberal way of thinking, "a tendency to oppression"; and it was for this reason as much as for any other that he welcomed the first mowing-machine in October 1831.

To Loudon, the mechanical mower, like railway transport and the penny post, was an evident mark of progress. We of a later age have grown a shade more sceptical. How few, to us, seem the unmixed blessings among machines. The steam-engine was a mistake—as the civilised Alexandrians had the wit to see. But in more modern times we have been blessed with the bicycle, the typewriter, the safety-razor, and, a little earlier than these, the lawn-mower.

Yet the inventor of the lawn-mower never achieved fame, as did the inventor of the safety-razor. You may seek in vain for the name of Budding in the *Dictionary of*

National Biography—a work whose columns are all too often closed against gardeners. He was christened Edwin, but in contemporary references he is just the "Mr. Budding", or more often "Budding" without the mister, who in 1830 patented a "machine for cropping or shearing the vegetable Surface of Lawns, Grass-plots, &c."

To some extent, Budding's machine was rather an adaptation than a new invention; for an apparatus more or less similar was already in use for cutting the pile on certain kinds of cloth. All the same, Mr. Edwin Budding surely deserves more credit than he has ever got for so greatly extending the application of a principle.

The first lawn-mower was manufactured to Budding's specification early in 1831 by John Ferrabee at his Phoenix Foundry near Stroud; and before the end of the next year similar machines were being produced by James Ransome of Ipswich. Twenty years later Messrs. Ferrabee and Messrs. Ransome showed the only two lawn-mowers at the Great Exhibition. They were almost identical with the original; and indeed the earliest mowers were very similar to our present-day machines.

Budding himself was delighted with his invention. "Country gentlemen," he says, "may find, in using my machine themselves, an amusing, useful, and healthy exercise." But the machines were made in two sizes, and a certain Mr. Merrick, writing to Loudon from Cirencester in September 1831, remarks: "I have had one of Budding's machines in use, when the grass required it, all this year, and am highly pleased with it. The narrow machine is best for a gentleman who wishes to use it himself, but the wide ones are preferable for workmen." The price of the small mower was seven guineas, of the larger one ten. And Loudon expressed the "sincere hope that every gardener whose employer could afford it would procure a machine and give it a trial".

The large machine seems to have been somewhat heavier, but not much less efficient than the ordinary fourteen-inch non-motorized mower of today. Its chief defect was the comparative frequency with which its blades required sharpening. Mr. Curtis, head-gardener at the London Zoo, calculated that "with two men, one to draw and another to push, the new mower did as much work as six or eight men with scythes and brooms".

Yet in spite of the machine's obvious advantages, there was, in this revolution on the lawn, as in others elsewhere, a conservative party that resisted change. Though conservatives may generally be right, this time they were wrong. There was much correspondence and controversy, and in controversy the correct gambit is to demonstrate as defects what your opponent claims as merits. One of the merits of the mechanical mower was, as we have seen, that it was at its best on dry grass. Accordingly we find a gardener in Chiswick writing that "mowing machines cannot well be used in wet weather, the cutter being apt to clog, and in such weather grass requires more frequent mowing".

By 1862, however, the mechanical movement was gaining momentum. In that year Edward Kemp, a professional landscape gardener, compelled to make economies in his ambitious plans for suburban gardens, tried to show that a "lawn is, on the whole, less expensive to keep up than flower-beds and borders, and should therefore abound where economy of keeping is sought". And he goes on to suggest that "in comparison with the use of a scythe, the saving from the employment of a mowing-machine will be very considerable". By about this time also, the earliest horse-drawn mowers were in use at Kew; and Dean Hole tells of a gardener at Rochester asylum who harnessed seven madmen to his machine. In the early eighties a Mr. R. Kirkham devised a mower propelled by a pedal-driven tricycle attachment, but this, even at the height of the cycling vogue, failed in popularity. More successful but not much more, was Mr. Sumner's one-and-a-half-ton steam-driven mower, patented in 1893.

However, Edward Kemp was, of course, right. When once it had proved itself and had overcome initial inertia, mechanical mowing greatly increased the number and extent of lawns, until just before the last war it was calculated that lawn grass covered more than seventy-five per cent. of the total garden area of England.

As a saver of time and trouble, gardeners are in fact immeasurably indebted to Mr. Budding. Nevertheless, as against the conservative man, the progressive-minded man is never content. Pushing a mower up and down in the sun is perhaps nearer to drudgery than making graceful sweeps with a scythe ever was, and even a motor-mower entails some mess, worry, and expense to keep it going. If only a lawn could be devised which would stay short without any mowing at all! From time to time much thought was given to this problem. In some places there are, or were till lately, broad moss walks 200 years old. But moss only grows well in semi-shade. Later, small areas of lawn have been fairly successful when laid down in the low-growing, sweet-smelling thymes. But thyme is a capricious plant, and such lawns are difficult to maintain.

In Ireland I have seen a lawn entirely composed of Mediterranean sandwort, *Arenaria balearica*—that "most beautiful of terrible weeds", as Farrer called it—and this was delightful in damp weather and never needed mowing. But, given a short drought such as even Ireland sometimes endures, and the green lawn was gone with surprising speed, leaving only a dry brown desert of withered sandwort.

There was one other notable effort in this direction.

In their Spring Catalogue for 1859, Messrs. E. G. Henderson and Son, a firm of nursery gardeners, made exuberant claims for *Spergula pilifera* or spurry as "a perfect substitute for grass lawns in villa gardens without mowing". "Maintaining," as they said. "its verdant freshness alike beneath storm and sunshine, this plant combines every needful feature of adaptation with economy, and a uniform aspect of neatness with the least possible care and attention". Nor was this all. With the nurseryman's well-known enthusiasm. Messrs. Henderson proceed:

> "Its fertility in bloom during the month of July is beautiful, it being at that period studded over with myriads of low, compact, salver-shaped, snow-white blossoms, appearing not as in fancy, but in reality, the living picture of an emerald-green velvet carpet spangled with innumerable stars."

Who would not abandon his mowing-machine for such a paragon among plants, notwithstanding that these were offered to the public—especially to "every lady amateur cultivator"—at two and sixpence a piece.

The pretensions of *Spergula pilifera*, as put forward so poetically by Messrs. Henderson and Son, were thoroughly tested by that good Victorian gardener, Shirley Hibbard. His early reports were cautiously favourable, and both seeds and plants were widely advertised. But somehow this spurry, which belongs to the same family as the sandworts, did not stay the course; and probably for the same reason—that it would not stand dry weather.

And so the no-trouble lawn had not arrived after all. And one must suppose that there is little use in looking for it; that this, like all other seekings after perfection—the quest of the Philosopher's Stone, or the Elixir of Life

—that this also is a vain thing. The price of a beautiful lawn, one of Spenser's "fair lawns to take the sun in Season due", is and most likely ever will be an all-too-frequent mowing through at least six months of the year. But it might have been worse. Let us thank heaven for Budding.

And surely what labour we endure is well spent. We may hope that it keeps us fit. And, looking beyond the merely physical, we may agree with Vicesimus Knox that "Few objects are more pleasing than a smooth lawn"; or, preferring Francis Bacon and his four green acres in a princely garden, that "nothing is more pleasant to the eye than green grass kept finely shorn".

ENVOY TO A BOOK ON GARDENERS

John Claudius and his Jane, alas too soon
By grave spade parted; William Robinson
Grafting more orchards near his hundredth year;
Farrer, flower-seeking on far mountain slopes,
Finding at Valley's End the Elysian Fields
And gathering there for ever fairer flowers;—
These planted gardens, and (implicit praise)
Their gardening prospered, Priapus-inspired
And by Anèmone breathed lightly on.

    And now, from one for those false quantities,
From all for anything impertinent
Impudent or improper that I've written—
Having the wit to know they gardened greatly—
I beg a ghostly pardon in good faith.

G. T.